Architectural Guide
Sarajevo

Architectural Guide
Sarajevo

Edited by LIFT Sarajevo

Nedim Mutevelić, Irhana Šehović, Dunja Krvavac,
Jasmin Sirčo, Senka Ibrišimbegović, Irfan Salihagić,
Edin Sarić, Farah Zubović, Zerina Salketić, and Edin Zoletić

With further contributions by Hubert Klumpner
and Michael Walczak

DOM
publishers

Historical Sarajevo
Page 40–51

Explore on foot

Formal Sarajevo
Page 52–117

Explore by bicycle, tram, bus, or car

Informal Sarajevo
Page 118–191

Explore on foot or by bicycle or car

Wider Sarajevo
Page 192–225

Explore by car

Contents

Sarajevo Old Town, view towards the west (2017)

Stojan Anzulović

Sarajevo New Town, view towards the west

Sarajevo Town Hall, view towards the north

Introduction

This guide aims to highlight Sarajevo's modern/contemporary architecture of the present while also revealing the peculiarities that draw more and more tourists to the city every year. Without the intention of being a comprehensive summary or timeline of modern/contemporary architectural history, it focuses on present-day Sarajevo, which has been promoted through the Days of Architecture Sarajevo platform for the previous 15 years.

Due to the historical blending of multiple cultures, Sarajevo is often depicted on postcards as 'European Jerusalem' or 'between the East and the West'. In addition, Sarajevo is frequently linked to wars. This is where the Archduke Franz Ferdinand of Austria was assassinated in 1914, which served as the official start of the First World War. In the recent past, Sarajevo suffered the longest siege in modern military history (1,425 days) during the war from 1992 to 1995, which caused significant damage and devastation to most of the city's existing structures. On the other hand, the 1984 Winter Olympic Games provided Sarajevo with the historical drive that promoted both the city's development and its positive brand.

Most studies of Sarajevo's urban evolution and modern/contemporary architecture are based on these historical references and an understanding of the east-to-west linear configuration, where layers from various historical periods are horizontally aligned.

This guide intends to offer a different understanding of the city and its architecture and showcase the authenticity shaped by extreme natural and social environments, mountains and wars, climate change and the post-war transition, attractive landscapes and spontaneous tourism, high altitudes and urban life.

Selected projects and authors featured in this guide have been chosen from the Days of Architecture Sarajevo archive, which has been created through various public programmes over the years. The primary objective of curating this guide is to showcase the richness, diversity, and distinctive approaches of modern and contemporary architecture in Sarajevo.

In the selection process, the previous visibility and impact of the projects within the wider public and architectural community discourse were taken into account. Priority was given to projects that had previously garnered attention, whether through media coverage, awards, or public recognition, as these projects play a significant role in shaping the architectural dialogue and contributing to the evolving identity of the city.

The first two chapters, Historical Sarajevo and Formal Sarajevo, are commonly recognised zones and depictions of Sarajevo. With that said, Informal Sarajevo and Wider Sarajevo offer different understandings and experiences of Sarajevo inextricably linked to its topography and all the in-betweens.

Historical Sarajevo is about the city's history and beginnings as an urban settlement in the fifteenth century with Oriental influences (1462–1878) and European influences (1878–1918). Architecture before 1918 prevails in this zone, so this chapter does not showcase selected buildings. Nonetheless, it is a reference for understanding the city and possible influences on its modern / contemporary architecture, as conceptualised by Juraj Neidhardt and Dušan Grabrijan in *Architecture of Bosnia and the Way Towards Modernity*. As this chapter provides no selected projects for Historical Sarajevo, other publications and guides should be consulted for exploring this period further.

Formal Sarajevo follows the common understanding of the city as a linear configuration along the central axis of Sarajevo valley with its lowest altitude of around 550 metres above sea level. It runs along the River Miljacka and the main street, forming the first visual experience of Sarajevo when arriving from the airport and travelling towards the Old Town. In this area, you will find most of the freestanding, large-scale, modern / contemporary buildings.

Cemetery in the eastern part of the Old Town

Informal Sarajevo captures architecture from the Formal Sarajevo zone and its main city thoroughfare. This part of the city is built from the axis and up towards the Sarajevo hillsides. Here, the city responds to the topography in its peculiar ways, with its controlled and organically expanding typologies, urban and semi-urban quarters, ladder streets, terraced housing complexes, with regionally and topographically influenced modernist architectural works contributing to a vibrant Sarajevo visual appearance. This chapter showcases a heterogenous Sarajevo in terms of architectural approaches and geographical locations.

Wider Sarajevo encompasses the city's broad metropolitan areas outside its administrative and central urban zones. Wider Sarajevo stretches towards the high-altitude mountains characterised by severe climate conditions, as well as to the nearby towns and villages that gravitate towards the capital. Most sites in this chapter can be reached within 45 minutes of the city centre by car.

Jasej Strop/Dreamstime

From Modern to Contemporary City

Senka Ibrišimbegović

Sarajevo is a unique city in which the historical timeline is translated in urban and architectural form. You can easily follow the different epochs by walking along the river from east to west. The cultural identity of the city is shaped through its historical and geographical position. Situated at the crossroads of Occidental and Oriental civilisations as well as of Continental European and Mediterranean cultures, Bosnia and Herzegovina, as well as its capital, has undergone a radical transformation of its socio-political organisation and has been subject to numerous rapidly established influences. Powerful empires and major cultural and political centres influenced the construction and reshaping of social awareness of the city and country. The cultural identity of specific regions affected their architecture, representing an inevitable and continuous process of symbolic identification with territorial and memory significance. Modern architecture in Sarajevo embodies a synthesis of modern and traditional thought and arises from a challenging cultural context, with a focus on the period following the First World War when

Midhat Mujkić/Studio Nonstop

Bosnian architects developed a distinct architectural language emphasising functionality and simplicity. The foundations of modern tendencies were inscribed in the work of local architects who were educated in Central European cultural centres or influenced by architects who migrated to Bosnia and Herzegovina. Among the pioneers promoting revolutionary changes in architecture design within the Bosnian context were Dušan Smiljanić and Helen Baldasar, who worked as teachers at the Technical High School in Sarajevo beginning in 1924. They provided encouragement and support for young architects returning to the country after graduating from Prague Academy, such as brothers Reuf and Muhamed Kadić, Emanuel Šamanek, Leon Kabiljo, and Jahiel Finci. Their works promoted international functionalism alongside high social awareness.

The process of urban transformation and architectural interventions in Sarajevo mainly entailed integrating new residential, cultural, and administration structures within the pre-existing Ottoman and Austro-Hungarian urban framework, given the city's limited town planning and infrastructure initiatives. Consequently, from the 1920s until 1939, the most significant architectural creations were individual buildings. Notable examples include the <u>Red Cross Building (1928–1929, Helen Baldasar)</u>, with a cinema hall, and the Kadić brothers' Pension Fund building. Architects Kabiljo and Finci's residential building with a steel and glass façade, <u>Obala Kulina Bana Residential Building (1939, Jahiel Finci, Leon Kabiljo)</u>, represented a novelty in Bosnian architecture of that time. Additionally, Viennese-educated architect Mate Baylon designed numerous

Marijin Dvor area, view towards the National Museum of Bosnia and Herzegovina, the Historical Museum of Bosnia and Herzegovina, and the Importanne Centre

public buildings such as banks, schools, and residential buildings. The architectural endeavours of Muhamed and Reuf Kadić in Sarajevo exemplified the integration of contemporary architectural, technological, and visual elements, thereby establishing the groundwork for new trends in modern and contemporary Bosnian and Herzegovinian architecture. These trends drew inspiration from heroic sources of modern art, machine aesthetics, and disciplined research within the field. They were also combined with a philosophy and sensitivity towards the cultural and natural context, encompassing values of the local heritage. This synthesis gave rise to buildings and urban ensembles of immense aesthetic and historical significance. The fusion of cultures in this approach fostered a unique perspective that honoured local cultural elements, integrating them within the principles of modernism. Between the two world wars, Marijin Dvor became a site for experimentation with the new principles of architecture and urban planning; in particular, with reference to the new

residential district Crni Vrh, according to the master plan from 1932. This represented a rather audacious technical experiment, bearing in mind it was complex terrain that the Austro-Hungarian administration avoided building on. Even more significantly, it was the only urban district where luxurious villas had been built according to the principles of the modern movement in Bosnia and Herzegovina, in which Stjepan Planić, among other important architects of that period, experimented with the translation of traditional architecture into modern forms.

During the second half of the twentieth century, Marijin Dvor again became the place of expression of architectural and urban planning avant-garde. In this context, the inevitable figure is Juraj Neidhardt, a student of Peter Behrens and a colleague of Le Corbusier, who significantly contributed to the architectural landscape of Bosnia and Herzegovina by arriving in Sarajevo in 1938 and establishing a theoretical foundation for local functionalism. Juraj Neidhardt's Marijin Dvor urban plan was accepted at the

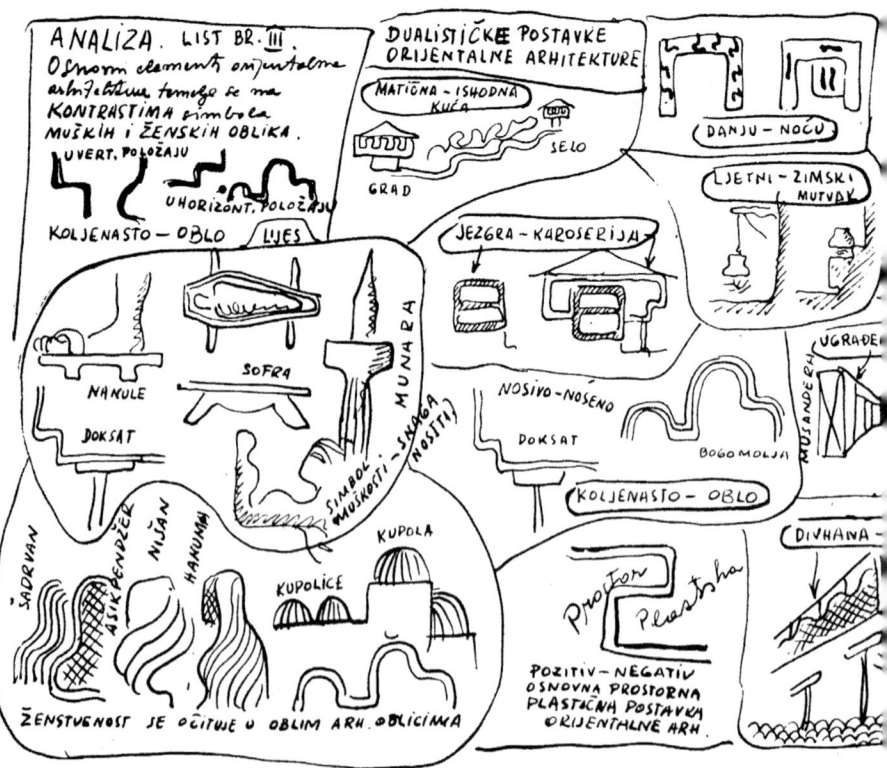

Architecture of Bosnia and the Way Towards Modernity, Grabrijan and Neidhardt, 1957

competition in 1955. His solutions, in a combination of the ideas of Le Corbusier and CIAM with certain elements of the architecture of Bosnia and Herzegovina, represent the continuity of architecture on its way towards modernity. Two years later in 1957, in collaboration with Dušan Grabrijan, Neidhardt published a book on Bosnian architecture titled *Architecture of Bosnia and the Way Towards Modernity*. This significant research emphasises the importance of traditional elements incorporated into principles of the modern movement. Neidhardt also designed the Parliamentary Assembly of Bosnia and Herzegovina (1982, Juraj Neidhardt), which established a new spatial trend for Marijin Dvor development in the city. Alongside Juraj Neidhardt and Dušan Grabrijan, Reuf and Muhamed Kadić laid the foundations for the modern architectural trends in Bosnia and Herzegovina. From the late 1960s to the mid-1980s, a mature modern architectural production emerged, characterised by the establishment of the Faculty of Architecture and Faculty of Civil Engineering (1950,

Jovan Korka, Emanuel Šamanek). The movement established at that time comprised two parallel discourses of architectural thought and approach. The first one, represented by institutional architects such as Ahmed Džuvić, Enver Jahić, Mirko Ovadija, Nedžad Kurto, and Amir Polić, focused on developing regional expression with distinct contemporary artistic expression. The second discourse was more internationally oriented, primarily manifested through public buildings designed by architects such as Ivan Štraus, Vladimir Dobrović, Zdravko Likić, Dušan Đapa, Živorad Janković, Milan Kušan, Branko Bulić, Hamdija Salihović, Halid Muhasilović, and Bogoljub Kurpjel. Architects Ivan Štraus and Zlatko Ugljen transcended geographical boundaries with their architectural contributions, exerting a profound influence on contemporary architectural trends across their entire nation from the 1960s onwards. Their work serves as exceptional examples of the universal legacy of modern architecture and the core principles of modern philosophy. These principles

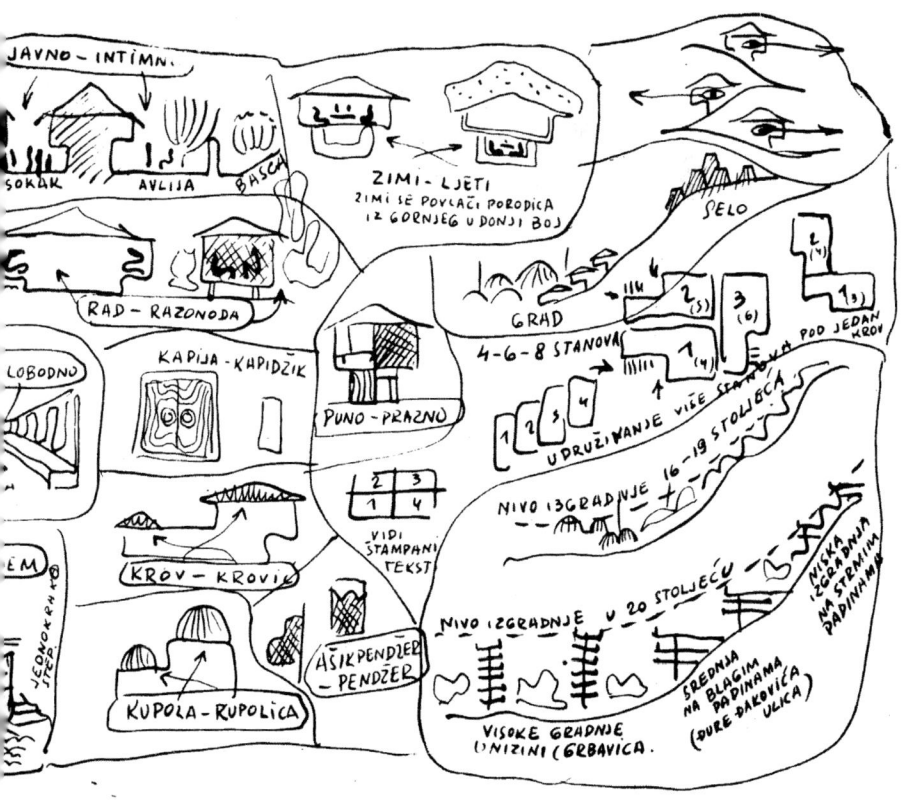

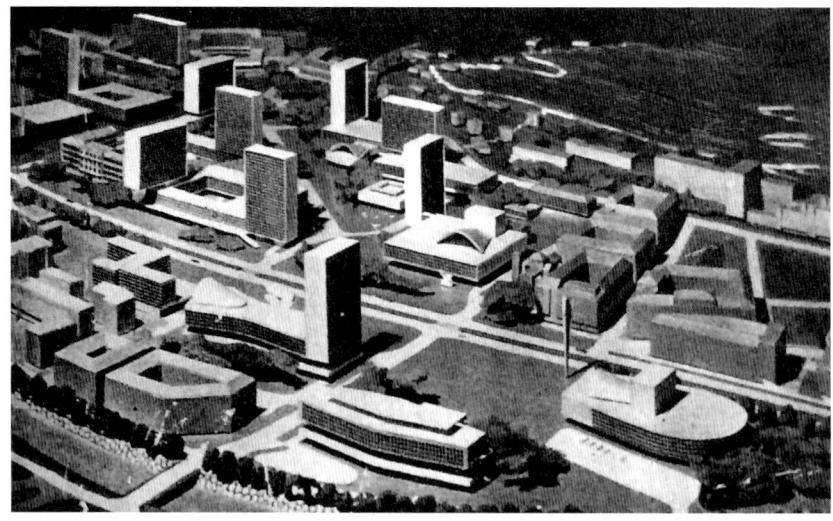

Model of Marijin Dvor, Sarajevo, third version of the urban plan in 1955 by Juraj Neidhardt

embrace the aesthetics of a 'machine for living', along with the notion that social and technological progress are inseparable. Štraus designed the Holiday Inn Hotel (1981–1983, Ivan Štraus), which served as the Sarajevo Olympic hotel, and the UNIS Twin Towers (Unitic Towers; 1986–1987, Ivan Štraus), both located in Marijin Dvor in Sarajevo. Zlatko Ugljen occupied a unique position with his research-oriented approach towards a new discourse of multi-layered, sculptural reinterpretation of space, embodied by Šerefudin's White Mosque in Visoko, (1969–1979, Zlatko Ugljen), which won the Aga Khan Award in 1983.

Over the past 27 years, the architecture of Bosnia and Herzegovina, particularly Sarajevo, has reflected the post-war and transitional period following the 1992–1995 aggression, as well as the neo-liberal social, cultural, and economic contexts of the general degradation of previous achievements and deregulation of public space. Modernisation processes and architecture development up to the early 1990s are considered an inseparable part of the nation's cultural heritage, rich with positive experiences but now unjustly neglected. The process of forming cultural identity has since then lost its original characteristics and become a medium for particular scheduled interests. Both returning to a nationally-oriented society and the unselective dictatorship of capital have almost eliminated the values achieved by architectural modernisation processes. Consequently, post-socialist modern society tends to erase established values of many historical architectural examples, leading to the potential disappearance of links in the continuity of cultural identity. This problem is further exacerbated when present contexts cannot generate quality new architecture. The challenge

Ars Aevi Museum designed by Renzo Piano

University Library designed by Adnan Pašić

is to find a good approach on how to direct the city's contemporary architecture urban planning to develop and materialise in a positive manner. Economic and social transition development brought to Sarajevo new functional programmes and a new urban and architectural identity, dominantly expressed by commercial facilities. Marijin Dvor again serves as a playground for the architectural experimentation of the epoch, featuring new dominant shopping centres such as Sarajevo City Centre (2014, GrupaARH, Sead Gološ) and Alta Shopping Centre (2005–2010, Studio Nonstop, Sanja Galić-Grozdanić, Igor Grozdanić). They also designed a hybrid building, Importanne Centre, (2005–2010, Studio Nonstop – Igor Grozdanić, Sanja Galić-Grozdanić). The three shopping structures stand out along the main traffic axis, and they symbolically reflect the values of a society in transition at the present time. In response to this reality, Marijin Dvor has yet to reveal its encapsulated yet unfinished cultural potential. It is also home to notable buildings including the National Museum of Bosnia and Herzegovina, from the Austro-Hungarian period, and the unique Historical Museum of Bosnia and Herzegovina (Museum of Revolution; 1958–1963, Boris Magaš, Edo Šmidihen, and Radovan Horvat), whose architecture epitomises the spirit of modernism. Its formal expression is rooted in the disciplined adoption of modernist procedures,

extending beyond the realm of architecture and into the broader sphere of culture. Adjacent to this museum, the City and Canton of Sarajevo dedicated a site for the Ars Aevi, Museum of Contemporary Art Sarajevo (since 1999, RPBW, Renzo Piano). Once built, the Ars Aevi Museum will reflect not only a form of contemporary architecture, but a whole philosophy and the idea to introduce contemporary art and architecture in the treatment of public spaces with great value and potential to create a better environment for the city of Sarajevo. In this context, Renzo Piano also designed a pedestrian Ars Aevi Bridge (2002, RPBW, Renzo Piano) connecting the residential area of Grbavica with the future museum complex. It was constructed in Italy and brought to Sarajevo in 2001. The whole area holds significant potential to become a new cultural / museum district in Sarajevo, featuring a vast public space between these buildings from which both visitors and residents would benefit. Construction of the Ars Aevi Museum progressed until 2021 when new energy emerged to finalise the main design project and raise funds for construction. Just across from this site to the north, a new master plan for the university campus is being developed by ARUP London. This area of the former military camp, known as Tito's Barracks, was granted to the University of Sarajevo after the siege. The campus is to be divided into three large zones. The

Master plan of the University of Sarajevo campus by ARUP London, 2022

eastern zone, right next to the United States Embassy, will contain buildings limited to 10 metres in height, among them the modern University Library designed by Adnan Pašić. Common university and student spaces are planned in the central zone as the new University Park. The western zone is planned to include the rectorate, an underground amphitheatre, a technological and incubation centre, a botanical garden, and a whole series of common student facilities. The new vision is to create an 'open campus' for all students, visitors, and residents, which will play a completely different role in the city.

Potential in Contemporary Architecture Development for the City of Sarajevo

As in the beginning of the twentieth century when revolutionary changes in architecture design were made with pioneers of the early modern movement, we can also say that in the beginning of the twenty-first century, we have a new possibility for revolutionary change in Sarajevo's urban and architectural development. A new threshold in the development of the contemporary architecture can be achieved with the construction of the Ars Aevi Museum of Contemporary Art Sarajevo, expected to begin in 2024. It is not only the building itself, but also the context of developing art and culture in the public space that hints that this architectural complex could become a generator for the development of the whole area. This design by Renzo Piano, one of world's best architects of this epoch, will have an international contemporary architectural impact in Sarajevo. Together with investing in the university campus, public buildings for education

US Embassy in Sarajevo, KCCT Architecture

and culture tend to be a good approach in making progress towards contemporary architecture development of Sarajevo. Culture in cities today is capitalised as a factor of social transformation and urban regeneration and an indicator of individual and collective well-being. Through culture and the processes that culture catalyses, cities can provide residents with new perspectives of participation in public life. It develops new mechanisms of solidarity and inclusion, revitalises, and gives colour to undeveloped areas, develops infrastructure, receives broader openness, and generates collaborations and partnerships that bring economic and social benefits to the entire community. Development of the city's cultural and spatial identity would be emphasised by creating a cultural / museum district in the area between the Historical Museum of Bosnia and Herzegovina, the future Ars Aevi Museum of Contemporary Art Sarajevo, and the National Museum of Bosnia and Herzegovina. The synergy between existing museum buildings and open public spaces represents the

potential that acts as a backdrop for future artistic experimentation and social cohesion. In this context, Marijin Dvor once again becomes a space where new revolutionary approaches are being tested and implemented, with respect to the positive practice in architecture and urban planning we have inherited from the past, especially lessons learned 'on our way towards modernity'.

References:

Ugljen-Ademović, N.; Ibrišimbegović, S. (2023, May). *An imaginary museum quarter: towards cultural and urban renewal.* In *Sarajevo Singular Plural* (pp. 295-306). Nomos Verlagsgesellschaft mbH & Co. KG.

Ugljen-Ademović, N.; Ibrišimbegović, S. (2016), *Creativity in Architecture as a Precursor of an Evolving Cultural Development – Case Study: Ars Aevi, Museum of Contemporary Art, Sarajevo, Bosnia and Herzegovina.*

Pašić, A. (2020). *Important phenomena of the modern and contemporary art and architecture of Bosnia and Herzegovina and the Bauhaus heritage - example of Sarajevo: Short survey.* In *The influence of the Bauhaus on contemporary architecture of Bosnia and Herzegovina* (pp. 70–93) National Committee of ICOMOS in Bosnia i Herzegovina

Picture taken above Mt. Trebević showing the bobsleigh track in the foreground and the city centre in the background

The Crumpled City

Nedim Mutevelić
Dunja Krvavac

Sarajevo's central and most densely populated areas are characterised by very few flatlands, packed up between steep mountainous terrain from the east and opening up towards the west. It is a city with brief visual perspectives, but always layered and extremely complex views that make it appear as a crumpled city. The vertical Z-axis in Sarajevo plays an important spatial-experiential role that is often neglected in urban analysis, descriptions, or tours through the city. However, descriptions typically concentrate on the XY-axes that follow the narrow space along the Miljacka riverbed, although due to its topography, the majority of the city is located on the high ground and hills that surround it. Experiencing the city is highlighted in its contrasts; ascents are followed by descents, narrow streets open up into wider boulevards, and small single-family homes transform into multi-storey high-rises – all revolving around the dynamic altitudes of the city and its surroundings. It is a similar experience to one you might have while visiting Innsbruck or Lisbon, which are both cities characterised by their mountainous terrains and backgrounds.

To understand the extent to which the city space is 'crumpled' and also significantly sloped, we can analyse the city's cross sections through some of the known or imagined transverse axes. This analysis reveals a very small perimeter of 'flat Sarajevo'. Starting from Vijećnica, City Hall (1894, Alexander Wittek, Ćiril M. Iveković), in the east, the width of the flat space runs along the Miljacka riverbed, starting at less than 50 metres on both sides of the river. Although Vijećnica is shaped like an equilateral triangle in its floor plan, seemingly out of context, its two sides are parallel with nearby hills, while its eastern peak corresponds to the intense topography of the eastern slopes of the Miljacka river canyon,

highlighting their positive-negative relationship. The air distance between Sarajevo Cathedral (1887, Josip Vancaš) on one side and the Papagajka residential building (1982, Mladen Gvozden, Dragan Bijedić, Architecture house Arhitekt) and Zvijezda Skyscrapers (1970s, Ivan Štraus) on the other side is less than 500 metres. The cathedral along with Štrossmayerova Street in front of it act as an anchor of the Central European urban matrix, with its north side straightened by the beginning of the hill. The perpendicular and symmetric relationship of the cathedral and Štrosmajerova Street is not achieved. The cathedral is slightly inclined, and the street slightly bends at its southern part. The Papagajka residential building (the 'Parrot Building' in English) is a large-scale, five-storey postmodernist building. It lies on the left bank of the Miljacka River and aligns with the Mjedenica Hill slopes on its south side, while the Zvijezda Skyscrapers ('Star's Skyscrapers' in English) have a specific position in the urban matrix, characterised by their close proximity to the slopes of Mt. Trebević and the lower scale Old Town, which makes their appearance unexpected and as if they are leaning onto the mountain.

A similar width of flat area continues until it reaches Alipašina Street and Hamze Hume Street, stretching up to the north along the 'green transversal' to the 10-hectare Olympic Complex with Asim Ferhatović Hase Stadium (1950, Vaso Todorović, Anatolij Kirjakov; 1984, Lidumil Alikalfić, Dušan Đapa), which has seats on slopes that follow the terrain configuration, and Olympic Hall ZETRA (1978–1982, Dušan Đapa, Lidumil Alikalfić), with a specific roof section as a transition between levels of the nearby transversal in the west and flat terrain of the complex. This section ends in the south with the Cultural and Sports Centre

Skenderija (1969, Živorad Janković, Halid Muhasilović, Ognjeslav Malkin), an iconic landmark tucked beneath the steep slopes of Mt. Trebević, marked by scattered housing on steep terrain.

Another slightly wider city cross section of relatively flat terrain is from Kovačići up to Crni Vrh. Starting with the narrow flat area of the 02 Residential Complex (1980, Hamdija Salihović) that is not related to topography but with two existing urban axes – the river and the road – the section bridges the Marijin Dvor area with the group of highest buildings in Sarajevo, the Parliamentary Assembly of Bosnia and Herzegovina (1982, Juraj Neidhardt),

Sarajevo City Centre (2014, Sead Gološ, GrupaArh), and Unitic Towers (1986–1987, Ivan Štraus), and continues up to the Residential Zone Crni Vrh (1933–1939, Mate Bajlon, Franjo Lavrenčić, Bruno Tartalja, Stjepan Planić, Danilo Kocijan, Franc Novak, Dušan Smiljanić). Settled on a hill with a steep terrain configuration towards the south, this residential zone was one of few planned in the period between the two world wars and is a certain milestone in the uprising of modern architecture and planning in the city. It is generally assumed that the architects of this residential zone were heavily influenced by European tendencies and international

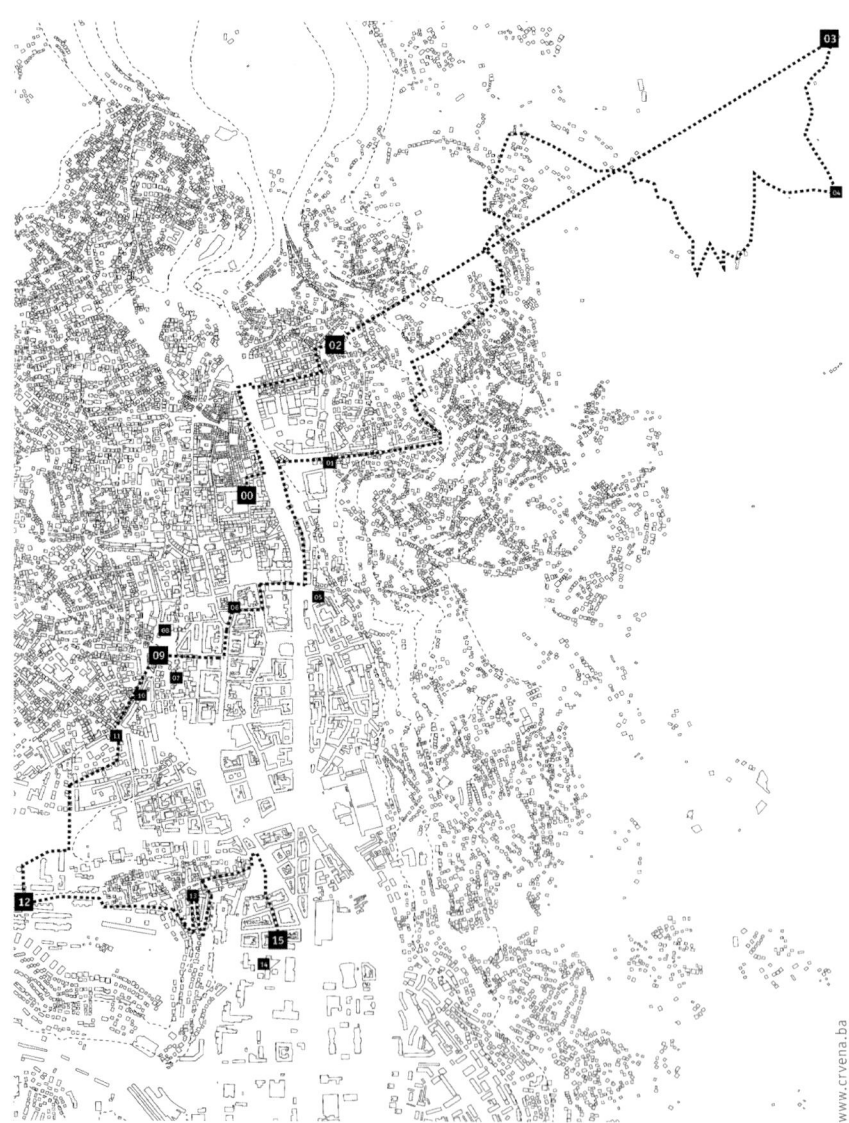

www.crvena.ba

The Crumpled City map by Dunja Krvavac and Nedim Mutevelić
for *Walks through non-fictional hoods* published by Crvena, 2022

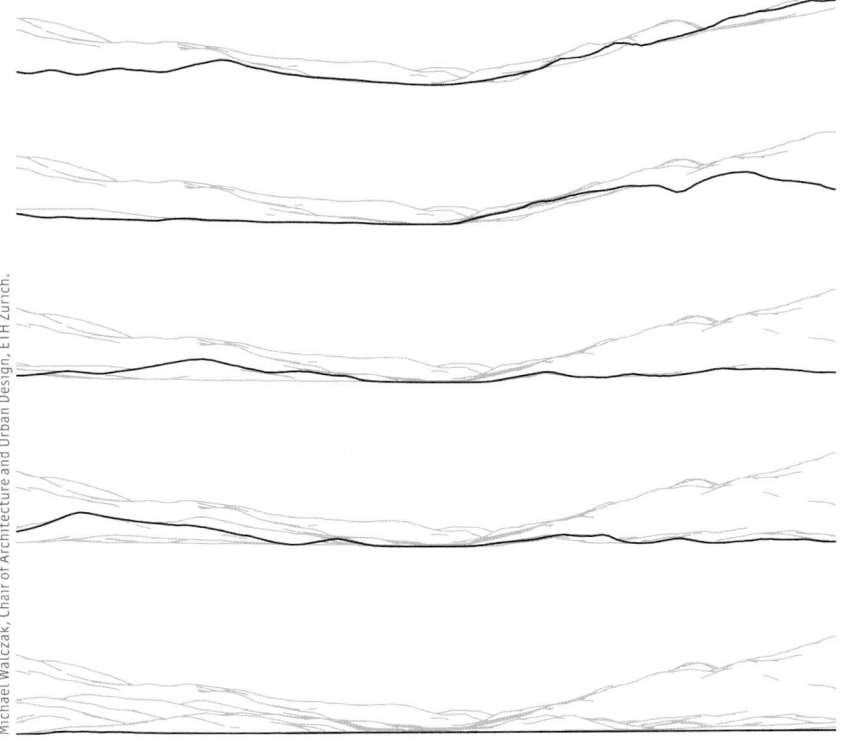

Michael Walczak, Chair of Architecture and Urban Design, ETH Zurich.

Wide cross sections of Sarajevo and its surroundings

style in terms of rational parcelisation and the proportions between public and private zones, while also incorporating traditional unwritten rules of Sarajevan *mahalas* in terms of organic links between green zones and houses and the 'right to the view and insolation' – a term coined 20 years later by Dušan Grabrijan and Juraj Neidhardt in the book *Architecture of Bosnia and the Way Towards Modernity*.

Just next to this Residential Zone Crni Vrh lies the uniquely planned serpentine street with five turns that easily explain its former name, Vijuge ('Curves' in English). Built at the turn of the nineteenth century with a large group of Central European villas tucked into the steep terrain, the street climbs up over 30 metres in 68 metres air distance, making the average inclination of the cross section 40 per cent.

Moving further to the west, a cross section between Kovačići Hill and Velešići Hill with a <u>Railway Station (1947–1952, Group of Czechoslovakian architects, Bogdan Stojkov, Lorenc Eichberger, Jahiel Finci, Muhamed Kadić, Emanuel</u> <u>Šamanek, and Dušan Smiljanić)</u> flat area becomes slightly wider for a total of 1.2 kilometres. As the rail track curve follows the ending contours of Hum and Velešići hills from west to the north, the building of the Railway Station stretches as a tangent line. The centre and two wings are slightly curved in a mirror to emphasise the relationship to the large (and possibly largest) flat urban plaza in Sarajevo, envisioned to extend over the only planned diagonal axis in Sarajevo, through Franca Lehara Street, between the <u>Holiday Inn Hotel (1981–1983, Ivan Štraus)</u>, the <u>Alta Shopping Centre (2005–2010, Studio Nonstop – Sanja Galić-Grozdanić, Igor Grozdanić)</u>, and <u>Sarajevo City Centre (2014, Sead Gološ, GrupaArh)</u>, ending up with a view towards the green top of Mt. Trebević.

From this point on, the similar cross sections with a flat area of 1–1.5 kilometres continue all the way to the Nedžarići and Stup, where they expand significantly into Sarajevo Field (Sarajevsko Polje).

These facts shed a different light on a number of city design issues. The very

Sketch of Sarajevo from the book *Architecture of Bosnia and the Way Towards Modernity* by Dušan Grabrijan and Juraj Neidhardt, 1957

small dimensions of the perimeter of a flat city explain why open public spaces – squares and parks – are of relatively small dimensions and the source of one of the key problems of spatial design and city development. A vast number of sidewalks are tight, even for one person, and show that they were not designed with the inclusivity of all demographic groups in mind. Therefore, in the zone outside the flat perimeter, architecture is mostly determined by the relationship with the terrain on which it is created.

The cable car, first built in 1959 and rebuilt in 2018, was the answer to overcoming the extreme verticality of the city. Sarajevo's average altitude is around 550 m above sea level – the lower cable car station is around 600 m above sea level, while the upper station is at 1,160 m above sea level. Overcoming more than 500 m in just 11 minutes highlights the importance of the cable car as a means of public transport. Due to the city's tightness in the flatlands, very few classic green public spaces were designed in the city itself, so it was important to think outside the box and embrace the surrounding nature to fulfil the needs of the city for green open public spaces.

Veliki Park is a 'park on the hill' – a characteristic natural cross section with a significant terrain slope. It is, therefore, an adjustment to the slope, largely organic and bumpy, to introduce the newer intervention of stairs in Veliki Park (2013, Nermina Zagora, Dina Šamić, Firma) that were designed to commemorate the liberation of Sarajevo in 1945. Not only do they overcome the altitude difference, but they also create a small seating area midway between its lowest and highest point, highlighted by public lighting that underlines the importance of safe public spaces. In its immediate vicinity, we find a distinctive architectural example in the Sun Housing Complex (1972, Ivan Štraus), which establishes a clear dialogue with the terrain. The terraces follow the topography, as well as the movement of the sun,

Sketch of the Sun Housing Complex by Ivan Štraus, 1971

opening to the south-west. In their rhythmic, layered composition, they reflect the philosophy of Bosnian oriental houses, mandating enough sunlight, a view outside, as well as privacy and garden spaces. On the other hand, At Mejdan Park is the only completely flat park because it is located directly and longitudinally along the river. The neighbouring Austrian Square is defined at its upper side by Vakuf Čokadži Hadži Sulejman (1938–1939, Reuf Kadić) as a free-standing modernist building, listed as a national monument of Bosnia and Herzegovina. From this building on, the slope, which increases significantly to the north following Bistrik Street and, with a short break next to the Old Bistrik Station, continues steeply up towards Trebević.

The Džidžikovac Residential Complex (1949, Reuf Kadić, Muhamed Kadić), one of the significant buildings of modern Sarajevo, represents a specific solution for the sloping terrain. It was designed as a series of linearly placed volumes that are height-adjustable to the terrain and follows the principle of the placement perpendicular to the contours of the slope. The entire complex consists of eight three-storey buildings in three rows divided into individual units by designing large terraces between the two buildings for the users of both buildings and with a large public green area in between.

Juraj Neidhardt also propagated the similar principle of relationship to the slopes both theoretically and in practice, as shown in two residential lamellas on a green slope in Alipašina Street – Alipašina Residential Complex (1952–1954, Juraj Neidhardt). The buildings are placed orthogonally towards the slope, which underlines the author's desire for the penetration of greenery into the space in between. Contrary to the previous practice of placing buildings linearly along the street, this spatial gesture dissolved the blocks and established the necessary green breaks that provoked better orientation of the apartments, ventilation, insolation, and movement through the neighbourhood, which clearly emphasises the entrance sequences, while at the same time covering the access to the buildings. Just 500 metres away from the Alipašina

Residential Complex, the hill from which the raw material for Sarajevo brickyards was extracted at the turn of twentieth century is home to the Ciglane Residential Complex ('Brickhood' in English; 1976–1989, Namik Muftić, Radovan Delalle). This complex with 1,451 residential units on a total area of 15.86 ha is the last major architectural engagement with a slope. During the design and construction process, the authors developed the term 'urban architecture' that represents a specific megastructure of continuous volumes designed according to place and time, at the same time allowing the users to be involved in the design process. Urban-spatial characteristics provided the construction of a neighbourhood inspired by traditional residential structures on the Sarajevo hills. The goal was to form different micro ambiences with views of Mt. Trebević, whereby a very important aspect was flexibility, especially on hillsides where larger structural spans were used. The approach is diametrically opposite to the design by Kadićs or Neidhart – instead of vertical forms, the design follows parallel to the slope on which it intervenes. The 'inclined elevator', which was included as an integral part of the settlement, can be read as an extrapolation of the cable car from today's perspective, with its arrival stop visible from the highest elevator stop.

In their book *Architecture of Bosnia and the Way Towards Modernity*, Dušan Grabrijan and Juraj Neidhardt described Sarajevo's structure as a city whose functional zones developed following its topography. The division of the city is well known: the flat and public part, the *čaršija*, where daily business is performed, and the hilly and more intimate part, the *mahala*, where people still predominantly live. It is also a known fact that *mahalas* developed organically, in agreement and in accordance with the terrain, leaving a significant mark on residential architecture. The climatic conditions characteristic of mountainous areas also influenced the design of housing units. These factors produced architecture entirely in accordance with the context and, at the same time, created to suit humans. Architecture became more than just space – it became a reflection of the development and progress of society. Grabrijan and Neidhardt describe this real picture of the city, but place it in a contemporary context and, for the first time ever, give us the opportunity to understand what life in a mountain city means. To illustrate, the upper stop of the Trebević cable car is located 1,160 m above sea level. If we walk, we climb to it through *mahalas* and settlements on the slopes of Trebević at altitudes of over 850 m. We have already reached the mountain at that point. For comparison, the highest populated place in Bosnia and Herzegovina – the village of Lukomir on the southern slopes of Bjelašnica Mountain – is 1,500 m above sea level. The surrounding mountains (Trebević, Jahorina, Bjelašnica, Igman) and their proximity were the main reason Sarajevo was selected to host the XIV Winter Olympic Games on 1 May 1978 ahead of Sapporo and Gothenburg. The organisation of the Games, which began in 1979, was followed by great momentum in the modernisation of the city, which continued after 1984. In addition to numerous sports facilities – Skenderija, Zetra, cable cars, ski lifts, the ski jump on Igman – several other facilities as well as numerous hotels and accommodation facilities were built, the airport was modernised, numerous façades in the city centre were refurbished, and the Olympic Villages of Mojmilo and Dobrinja were built from scratch.

Trebević was chosen as the site for a new bobsleigh track within the larger complex. The track was built based on Gorazd Bučar's design. It opened in 1982 as one of the fastest, steepest, and safest bobsleigh tracks in the world. One direct participant (Živorad Torlić) in the construction said of its qualities: 'It had the advantage of being the southernmost. Another advantage was that it is located almost in the city … And all the experiences from several Olympic tracks in Europe were collected – at that time, even 10 years after the construction, there was no better bobsleigh track in Europe.' With a total length of 1,300 m, the Trebević bobsleigh track has 13 curves, which, along with the ambience, make this facility significant on a global level among only 18 bobsleigh tracks around the world.

Today, Sarajevo has climbed high into the mountains that surround it. Some new neighbourhoods, villas, hotels, and restaurants emerged on the meadows and slopes – in an unplanned rather than planned manner. In the pursuit of income, much has been built with little regard for

belmac/iStock

Aerial view over misty Sarajevo

the meaning and enthusiasm of which Grabrijan, Neidhardt, and Le Corbusier spoke. The city stretched and expanded, but also fit into all the creases of the crumpled terrain. However, amid the haphazard growth and development, the messy topography of Sarajevo has undeniably created a unique and captivating atmosphere that has increasingly attracted tourists over the past decade. The city's crumpled landscape, with its charming, cobbled streets winding through hilly neighbourhoods has a magnetic appeal that enchants visitors from all corners of the globe. The juxtaposition of the flat and bustling *čaršija*, where daily business thrives, and the intimate and hilly *mahalas*, where locals predominantly reside, adds to the city's allure.

Sarajevo's architecture, moulded by its diverse topography, is a testament to the resilience and adaptability of its inhabitants. The challenging topography also presents a significant test for architects and urban planners. They are tasked with finding innovative solutions to harmonise the built environment with the crumpled terrain. This has led to the emergence of creative architectural designs and urban planning strategies that embrace the uniqueness of the city's topography.

Sarajevo, with its crumpled terrain and intricate urban fabric, has given rise to a distinctive atmosphere that acts as a powerful magnet for tourists. The city's architecture, shaped by its unique context, serves as a testament to the adaptability and ingenuity of its inhabitants throughout history. While presenting challenges to architects and urban planners, this topography has sparked innovation and creativity in design, resulting in a harmonious co-existence of built structures and natural surroundings.

Shaped by its crumpled character, Sarajevo and its architecture continue to enchant tourists, leaving an indelible impression and preserving the city's unique identity for years to come.

References:

Mutevelić, Nedim; Krvavac, Dunja (2022): *Architecture of the Crumpled City.* In *Walks through non-fictional hoods,* edited by Dugandžić, Danijela; Dugandžić, Andreja; Misaljević, Neven; Mraović, Boriša. Sarajevo, Association for Culture and Art Crvena

Grabrijan, Dušan; Neidhardt, Juraj (1957): *Arhitektura Bosne I Hercegovine i put u suvremeno.* Ljubljana, Ljudska pravica

Mutevelić, Nedim; Bošnjak, Katarina; Boriša, Mraović (2018): *3650 Days of Contemporary Architecture in Sarajevo.* Sarajevo, Buybook

The Urban Transformation

Hubert Klumpner
Michael Walczak

The urban transformations of Sarajevo engage with the people of Sarajevo, at the intersection of architecture, landscape, urbanism, design, and public art, envisioning radical trans-scalar processes and interventions, bringing together the cities' urbanisation, digitalisation, and ecologisation. Sarajevo´s culture is as diverse as its rich architecture and history of urbanisation. It is located on the 'Balkan Route', a crossroads between north and south, east and west.

Future design projects in Sarajevo could actively reimagine a new legacy at the intersection of home-grown turbo architecture. It raises the issue of resources on different scales and disciplines for the entire city and canton of Sarajevo, challenging the new standards of SDGs, IPCC reports, net zero, ESG evaluation, climate protection laws, and providing space for a culture of circularity, repair, and upgrade over time. Sarajevo is the arena of urban transformation on shifting scales. Like no other European city, it is opening up a discussion on constructing new frontiers of reactivating, reimagining, reurbanisation, reliving, redesigning, reconstructing, and regenerating what is already there, which is presented in this *Architectural Guide Sarajevo*.

Green and Climate Corridors

Traditionally, Sarajevo is read linearly from the east to the west in the direction of the valley. It starts from the Ottoman to the Austro-Hungarian and ends with the typical modernist, socialist, functionalist, and mono-functional urban fabric infrastructure. A re-structuring of Sarajevo's urbanistic reading was introduced by the first General Urban Plan (GUP) in 1965 and its upgrade in 1985 for the XIV Winter Olympic Games. The spectacle of the games accounted for the concentration of the events at a distance of fewer than 25 km from the city, making Sarajevo a total urban experience. Twelve transversal roads, including highways,

Aerial view over cloudy Sarajevo

bridges, and tunnels – still rooted in modernistic ideas of urban planning as traffic planning – tilted 90 degrees to the main longitudinal axis towards transversal connections. Today, these ideas actually became reality only in the valley bottom, while the majority of the proposed infrastructure remained imaginary projects in all official policy and planning documentations of the Canton of Sarajevo until now. Nevertheless, some unfinished ideas serve as moments of reinvention, such as the highway tunnel under the Ciglane Residential Complex ('Brickhood' in English; 1976–1989, Namik Muftić, Radovan Delalle), covered public events spaces, or the neighbouring unfinished bridges that have a popular market below. Future scenarios could reimagine the vision of transversals in the form of green and climate corridors, while green corridors are not only 'green' in terms of vegetation but also in terms of providing infrastructure, services, and connectivity across the whole valley. The future design challenge includes redesigning and densifying public open space, combining social and environmental developments into a system of architectural, urban, and landscape design networks. Linear multifunctional corridors can strategically connect to the immediate context and subcentres with feeder routes (considering Sarajevo's 'main axis'), participatory public spaces, markets, playgrounds, production, and create new eco-systemic connections with increased social and ecological qualities.

Mahale Hillside Settlements

The existing assemblage of different religions and ethnic populations requires translation in shared public indoor and outdoor spaces and a narrative of architecture and urban design in practice. We ask for an integration of the city's social, economic, and cultural redevelopment. Rooted back in the fifteenth century oriental phase, in the development of the city core as we know it today, the Ottomans established a typical oriental urban typology with functional zoning: the bazaar business district (*čaršija*) and residential districts (*mahalas*). As a particular urbanistic phenomenon, the *mahalas* include housing, mosques with cemeteries, bakeries, water fountains, and schools within walkable distances – a '15-minute city' in the current discourse. These typologies could conceptually serve for the decentralised reimagination of the wider hillside settlements in Sarajevo, including urgent

Michael Walczak

Michael Walczak

Market under an unfinished highway bridge, providing covered public space

Market combined with a shopping centre: BTC Merkur Shopping Centre (2011, Sead Gološ)

topics of public infrastructure such as energy and mobility. The hillside settlements originate from illegal housing construction after the First and Second World Wars and currently deal with issues such as energy supply, pollution, and access to public infrastructure. Sarajevo's current air pollution situation is caused by roughly 50 per cent individual traffic and 50 per cent individual home heating. Decentralised heat pumps, solar, and biogas could support the reduction of emissions as an alternative to the solid fuels commonly used in the hillside settlements, translating these observations into the basic thesis of constructing an

urban imaginary, creating an interplay of a linear public space system to provide identity and orientation in the Miljacka River valley of Sarajevo. The watershed of the Miljacka River, wells, fountains, retention infrastructures, and flood plains are the point of departure. They have the potential to unlock socio-ecological systems, multifunctional corridors, and catalytic projects that can transform fragmented neighbourhoods, offering an integrated living system of public water places for the inhabitants. Starting with demonstrators and scalable prototypes, a small-scale pilot project such as a water fountain introduced in the hillside

Aerial view over Sarajevo New Town

settlements and returning to the ideas of the *mahalas* could become an urbanistic project when linking to existing and future water and public infrastructure provision of the whole city and canton.

From Linear to Circular Burek Typology

Instead of reinterpreting the traditional longitudinal development axis of the valley of Sarajevo, future design tasks could redevelop and give a new reading of the development to the cross section of the valley, turning towards layers of interdependencies, juxtapositions of difference, and division in a cross section of the city. The design should focus on identifying an underlying logic that connects the valley's fragmented neighbourhoods, its topographical symmetries and asymmetries, and its natural and human-made divisions that simultaneously splinter and unify Sarajevo. The distinct topography and the dense settlements require alternative multi-modal modes of transport, considering all seasons throughout the year, from winter to summer. Circular rather than linear cable cars, with a small building footprint and intermediate stops that also allow the transportation of people, electric and non-electric bikes, goods and rubbish, and are connected to the existing public transport network, would allow for an integrated mobility and logistics system, conceptualised by the Sarajevo Canton Institute of Planning and Development as a circular 'ring rail' around Hum and Žuč mountains. The 'ring rail', metaphorically defined as 'burek', would allow the use of existing railways, formerly used by the Volkswagen Factory, connecting the settlements of Vogošća and Rajlovac.

Agent-based Sarajevo

Looking into population and migration dynamics and possible future scenarios, in the year 2013, the entire population of the Canton of Sarajevo, including all nine municipalities, was 409,375 according to the 2013 census. Looking at the four municipalities that make up Sarajevo city proper (Stari Grad, Centar, Novi Grad, and Novo Sarajevo), the population was 273,136. The population of the Canton of Sarajevo is expected to grow to 500,000 people by 2036. The municipality of Ilidža would then become the most populated municipality, rebalancing the

Sloven Anzulović, LIFT

population and services between the east and west city compartments, thereby allowing enhanced access to public services in western parts of the city. A population increase of 500,000 would necessitate a 34 per cent increase in the number of dwellings for a population increase of 17 per cent. This is due to different household structures. Past statistics and future trends regarding tourism also indicate higher arrival numbers, materialised by the increasing capacity of the current Sarajevo International Airport (1984, 2023, Sead Gološ, GrupaArh; extension). Further, to accommodate such population scenarios, concepts of decentralisation and the fostering of polycentric development could further disentangle the current centralised services and traffic situation to provide high-quality public and social services. Such scenarios and the further integration of new transversal connectivity would allow – partially or fully – to programmatically shift spaces for roads to alternative dynamic usage as public space for trees, bikes, scooters, and other forms of mobility.

Climate Action

Sarajevo is characterised by its unique topographical valley setting as well as its extensive water reservoirs, river streams, and side creeks, being exposed to both flooding and landslides. Historically, many open water surfaces were covered by infrastructure such as streets. The opening of these existing natural resources could further provide cold air streams and the cooling of the city, thereby contributing to the improvement of air quality – both important characteristics of the city's challenges. This phenomenon is defined as the process of 'daylighting' rivers and streams – literally providing natural sunlight to the water sources and their nature. Exhibitions in the National Museum of Bosnia and Herzegovina in Sarajevo communicate complex issues on science, technology, and policy and make them accessible to the general public through the arts. Alternative artworks are highlighting different forms of environmental pollution and climate change issues. The associated and amplifying inversion weather phenomena are related to the minor access of natural wind corridors and cooling as a result of the valley. However, interesting urbanistic climate-responsive examples emerged. For example, the Grbavica district in the Novo Sarajevo municipality shows the response of building volume and orientation towards wind due to its diverse building typologies, porosity, vegetation, and open and green spaces.

Four-dimensional Digital Twin

We are currently witnessing and participating in two realities: actual and virtual reality. The baseline of any real-time 4D (three dimensions and time) Digital Twin is mostly constructed by various types of data, particularly geo-referenced data (GIS) in planning. A brief discourse into Sarajevo's history allows us to understand the relationship between planning and digitalisation.

After the Second World War and as part of the Socialist Federal Republic of Yugoslavia, the Sarajevo Canton Institute of Planning and Development was founded in 1954 under the name 'Urban Planning Institute of the City of Sarajevo'. At that time, the preparation of the General Urban Plan of the City of Sarajevo had already begun. The architect Juraj Neidhardt (1901–1979), with his huge architectural oeuvre in Sarajevo, also worked in what was at that time the Urban Planning Institute of the City of Sarajevo, contributing to the General Urban Plan, with Marijin Dvor, and the regulation of Titova Street. In 1979, the Urban Planning Institute merged with the Institute for Economic Planning, which included the Institute for Informatics, integrating all aspects of urban life. In 1985, the Institute for Informatics separated from the Institute for City Development Planning, which grew into the Statistical Institute of the City of Sarajevo, while the Department for Socio-Economic Planning remains within the institute. Today, due to its informatics legacy, the Sarajevo Canton Institute of Planning and Development has a significant amount of data available to it, spanning from the census to infrastructure,

Alejandro Jaramillo Quintero, Michael Walczak, Hubert Klumpner

Raw coloured tie point cloud in Sarajevo, Buća Potok, Transversale 6

and all homogenous throughout the whole canton. Combined with automatised point-cloud data collection techniques using drones and a mobile outdoor research laboratory studio mobil / think tank station (2021–, ETH Zurich and Urbanthinktank next: Hubert Klumpner, Michael Walczak), Sarajevo could set the new AI (artificial intelligence) standard for urban planning and design in cities. The year 2024 marks a core moment in Sarajevo's planning legacy – along with the celebration of the 40th anniversary of hosting the Olympics and 70th anniversary of the Sarajevo Canton Institute of Planning and Development. The legacy is also present in the affinity of the younger generation towards virtual reality, software development, and coding. This could spark and incubate Sarajevo as the new 'Silicon Valley' or 'Silicon Hills' – also in terms of architectural and urban prototypes, visible in today's economic dynamics and start-ups such as the Ministry of Programming, Greenpark Symphony Office Building (2017–2020, Studio Nonstop: Sanja Galić-Grozdanić, Igor Grozdanić), or the IT Park Šip, and related projects such as the Roof Gardens Mixed-use Building (2019–2023, Studio Nonstop: Sanja Galić-Grozdanić, Igor Grozdanić + Filter: Nedim Mutevelić, Vedad Islambegović, Asmir Mutevelić, Kenan Vatrenjak, Ibrica Jašarević).

Laboratory for Small-scale Projects and the Never-ending Transformation

Designing integrated urban strategies and prototypical architecture projects on different scales in coalition with local stakeholders could define an urban paradigm based on a proactive approach. In the spirit of the K67 Kiosk (1967–, Saša Mächtig), Sarajevo offers a laboratory of powerful transformative processes and adaptive small-scale initiatives and designs. Sports fields were transformed into graveyards and later sites of monuments (Sportski Centar Kovači). Vilsonovo Šetalište Street is sometimes a street and sometimes a public space for pedestrians, bicycles / scooters, and street (food) vendors. Olympic Infrastructure such as the Olympic Complex and Olympic Hall ZETRA (1978–1982 Dušan Đapa, Lidumil Alikalfić) became a 'maker space' under the tribunes for local craftsmanship. The 'Ključ' Sock Factory was a space for production and economy in the city centre – as a new way the circular economy could be applied to other sectors such as waste management, food production, and processing. During World Rivers Day on 26 September 2021, the radical public action of using boats on the Miljacka River to collect water samples / probes and highlight the site of the former 'City

Beach' marked the historic river use of boats and public swimming pools close to the Miljacka River using its water supply, close to the 'Vijećnica' City Hall building, and was performed, filmed, and instantly screened in the Sarajevo 'Kino Meeting Point' as part of the Days of Architecture 2021 in Sarajevo. Sometimes permanent, temporary, mobile, and short-term strategies result in long-term value production.

What's Next?

Sarajevo has the power to search for its strategies rather than looking for *Vorbilder* ('role models') in the West (including scenarios of Bosnia and Herzegovina joining the European Union or EU) or the East (investment from China or the Middle East, and the discussion about the Belt and Road Initiative as the New Silk Road). The fundamental questions of any large-scale urban transformation event putting a city or an entire country on the world map, from the Olympic Games to Soccer World Cups or world exhibitions, are to what extent the event should be seen as temporary and to what way architecture designs extend to something more permanent. The thinking includes existing and new buildings and infrastructure. Durability becomes a concept that questions circularity, reuse, and resources, metaphorically and practically enhancing the city profile. How are the costs, benefits, (alternative) ownership, and land-use rezoning distributed to the citizens and the urban development, commercialisation, and media of events? How are these public and private ownership models expanding into the air rights and underground properties?

Small-scale projects and prototypical concepts are ready to be upscaled to the urban scale through policy recommendations, guidelines for urban rules, and general advice. In this spirit, we see prototypical ideas emerging. Red Bull is staging downhill biking and skating events on the former Winter Olympic <u>Bobsleigh & Luge Track (1982, Goražd Bučar, Živojin Vekic, Nebojša Krošnjar)</u> on Trebević Mountain, and it is imagined to transform the former <u>Olympic Hotel Igman (1983, Ahmed Džuvic)</u> on Igman Mountain into a Berlin-style nightclub. We will see how contemporary practices in Sarajevo engage in the development and transformation of the city and different ways to observe and engage with urban conditions in absorbing architectural culture into everyday realities in Sarajevo, the Western Balkans, and beyond. Practices of alternative figurations and the reimagination of urban transformation suspend linear thinking and the binaries of city and countryside into the extended turbo-reality of Sarajevo and the Western Balkans.

Michael Walczak

Vilsonovo Šetalište Street: Public space for pedestrians, bicycles / scooters, and street vendors

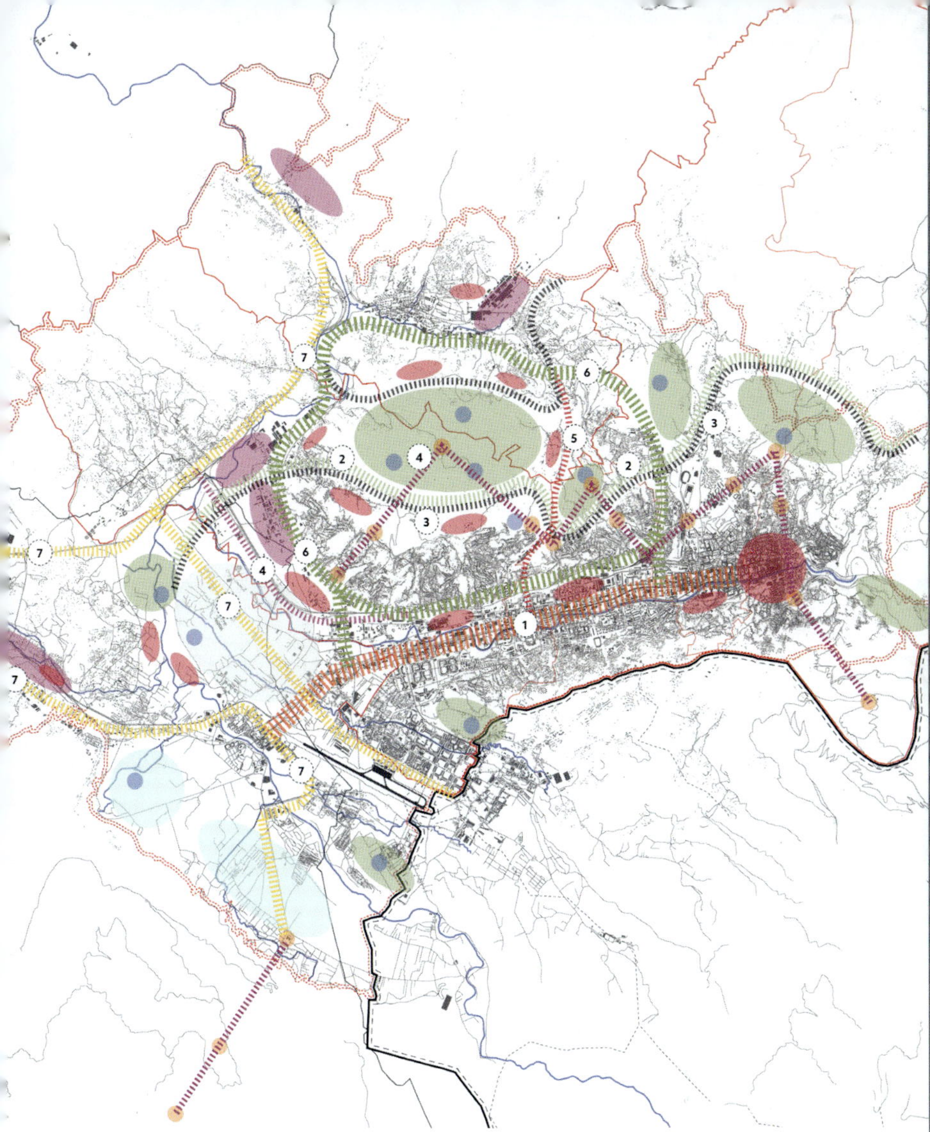

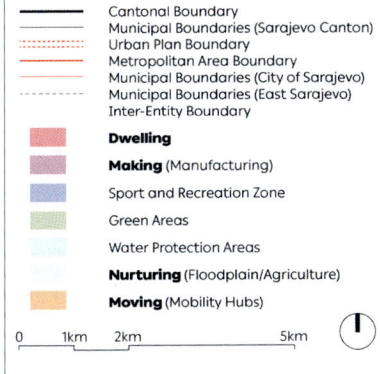

References:

Sarajevo Canton Institute of Development and Planning. <https://zpr.ks.gov.ba/zavod/o-zavodu> accessed 18 April 2023

Demographic Scenarios for the New Urban Plan for Sarajevo Canton: An Agent-based Digital Twin; Pagani, Marco; Viteškić, Vedad; Marini, Marcello; and Taletović, Jasmin; In 4th Conference on Urban Planning and Regional Development; 2023

Preparation of the New Urban Plan for Sarajevo Canton; Walczak, Michael; and Pelja-Tabori, Nataša; In 4th Conference on Urban Planning and Regional Development; 2023

Klearjos Eduardo Papanicolaou, Alejandro Jaramillo Quintero, Michael Walczak, Hubert Klumpner, ETH Zurich, Chair of Architecture and Urban Design. <https://vimeo.com/608104722/cd162a6966> accessed 12 April 2023

Srdjan Jovanovic Weiss; Turbo architecture

Scenarios of the New Urban Plan for Sarajevo Canton

———	Cantonal Boundary
– – –	Municipal Boundaries (Sarajevo Canton)
·········	Urban Plan Boundary
———	Metropolitan Area Boundary
– – –	Municipal Boundaries (City of Sarajevo)
– – –	Municipal Boundaries (East Sarajevo)
	Inter-Entity Boundary

▮	**Dwelling**
▮	**Making** (Manufacturing)
▮	Sport and Recreation Zone
▮	Green Areas
▮	Water Protection Areas
▮	**Nurturing** (Floodplain/Agriculture)
▮	**Moving** (Mobility Hubs)

0   1km   2km   5km

Source: Michael Walczak, Suzana Lepanović, Hubert Klumpner, Chair of Architecture and Urban Design, ETH Zurich

Historical Sarajevo

1

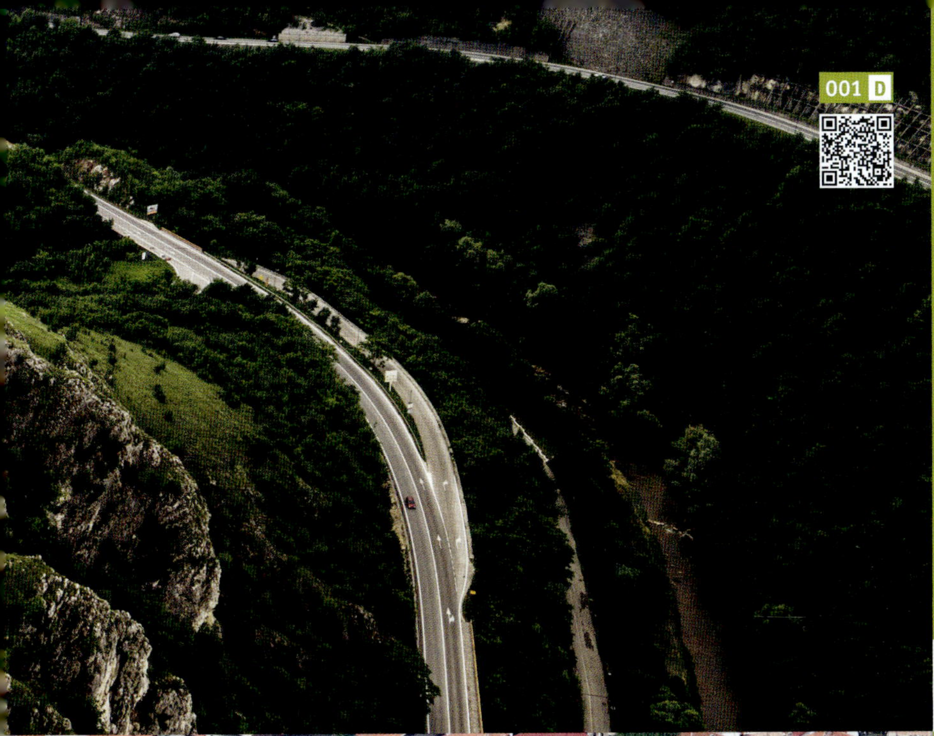

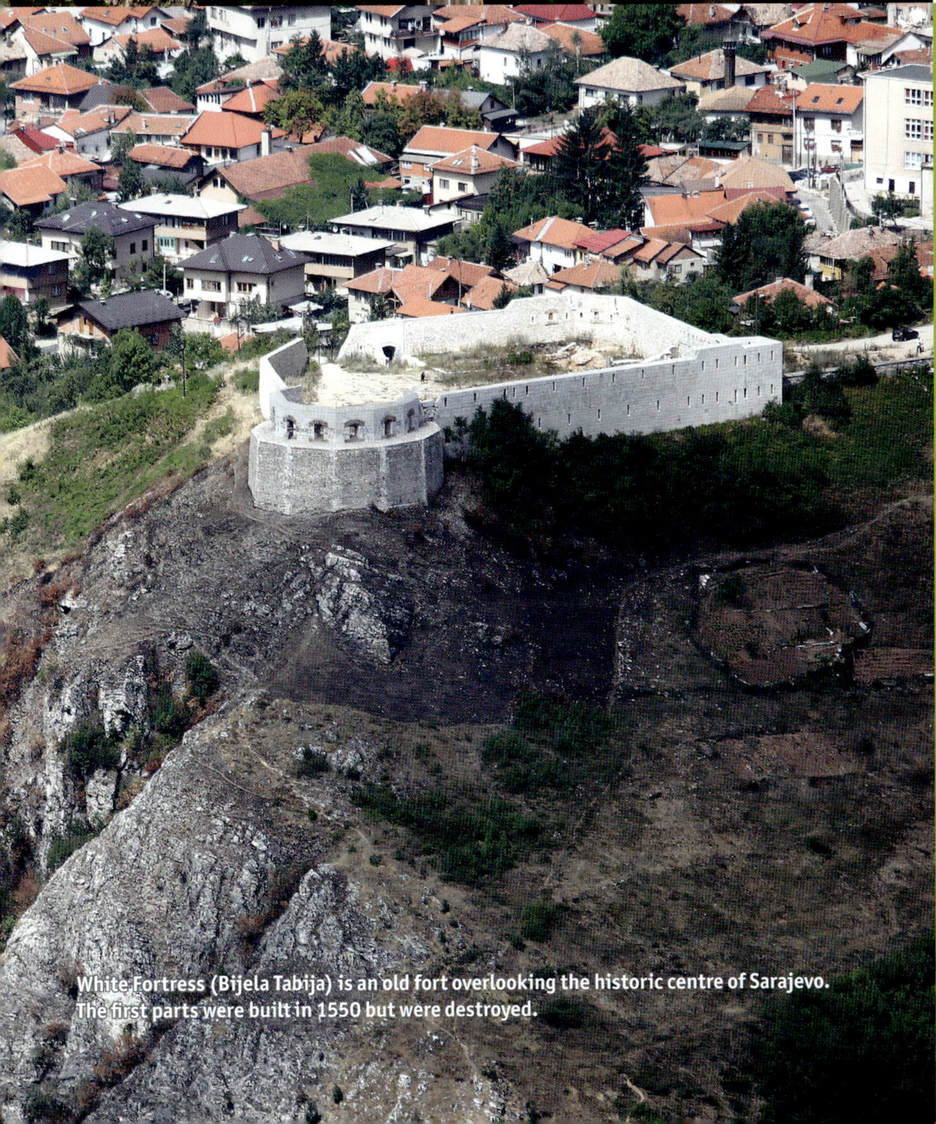

White Fortress (Bijela Tabija) is an old fort overlooking the historic centre of Sarajevo. The first parts were built in 1550 but were destroyed.

Aerial view of the oldest part of Sarajevo

Historical Sarajevo

Sarajevo's history as an urban settlement dates back to the fifteenth century, although the population of the Sarajevo valley has been documented since the Neolithic period. In Butmir, there was a significant settlement with 90 dugouts at that time. While the Copper Age did not leave traces of settlements, depots were found, indicating large movements of prehistoric groups. The Bronze Age saw the establishment of settlements, such as Illyrian gardens, strategically located on hilltops, which remained in use until the sixth century. The region experienced a high population during the Hallstatt second century BCE; the Romans conquered the Illyrian tribes, incorporating the region into the Dalmatian Province. Ilidža emerged as the administrative centre, evidenced by the variety and layout of archaeological finds. With the arrival of the Slavic peoples in the late seventh century, the ethnic structure of the population changed, and the Sarajevo valley became densely populated with a network of villages, predominantly agricultural.

The independent Bosnian Banate began forming in the twelfth century and Sarajevo became part of the Vrhbosna district. The Ottoman conquest of the region began gradually in the fifteenth century, capitalising on Sarajevo's advantageous position as a major crossroads with a healthy climate and an ample water supply. Unlike the concentric growth pattern seen in Western settlements, Ottoman-Turkish culture emphasised a strict differentiation between work and residency. The city expanded through the creation of smaller residential zones called *mahalas*, with free spaces gradually filled over time. The Waqf (Vakuf) institution and endowments of Gazi Isa-bey Ishaković played a significant role in establishing the city's functions, including mosques, *caravanserais*, *hamams*, bridges, stores, and water systems. Sarajevo's development continued along these lines, evolving into a robust industrial centre during the second half of the sixteenth century with the construction of significant structures endowed by Gazi Husrev-bey.

1

Judy Dillon/iStock

002 D

The Tašlihan: Ruins of a place for travellers built during Ottoman rule, sixteenth century

Under Austro-Hungarian rule from 1878 to 1918, Sarajevo experienced gradual territorial expansion mainly towards the West. It served as the capital of the Austro-Hungarian province of Bosnia and underwent significant transformations as it transitioned from a romantic oriental city to an industrial hub. The clash of opposing civilisations and the development of industries, particularly construction, utilities, and transportation, prompted the city's territorial border to shift significantly westwards.

Elenarts108 /iStock

003 D

The Evangelist church was designed by architect Karel Pařík in a Romanesque-Byzantine style and opened in 1899. Today it houses the Academy of Fine Arts Sarajevo (ALU).

004 C

visitsarajevo.ba

Saint Joseph's Church was also built by Karel Pařík, a successful architect in the Austro-Hungarian empire, but in the architect's later years from 1936 to 1939.

Philipp Meuser

005 D

Interior of Sarajevo Town Hall by architect Alexander Wittek (1894), destroyed in 1992 and reconstructed by Studio Urbing (1996)

The Olympic Museum Sarajevo

The eclectic-style *Villa Mandić* was built in 1903 by Czech-born architect Karel Pařík. The building has housed the Olympic Museum of Sarajevo since 1984.

1

Philipp Meuser

006 D

007 D

The Gazi Husrev-beg Mosque was built in 1531 by Persian architect Adjem Esir Ali

Between the two world wars, Sarajevo's architectural landscape experienced limited changes, with spatial interventions primarily focused on interpolation within the existing urban structure. The post-war period witnessed rapid growth, particularly towards the west following a longitudinal plan basis. The new city parts adhered to a progressive urban model aligning with the development of other cities in Yugoslavia.

Present-day Sarajevo covers nearly 2,000 square kilometres and had a population of 447,000 (10.8 per cent of the population of Bosnia and Herzegovina) according to the 1981 census. The tighter city area, spanning 486 square kilometres, accommodates 303,000 residents.

During the Oriental influences period (1462–1878), Sarajevo's architectural styles exhibited clear connections and stylistic affiliations with Islamic art in Turkey. Ottoman architects who were responsible for constructing monumental objects during the sixteenth-century Classical period contributed to this connection. The city showcases semi-domed constructions as the pinnacle of artistic expression in the Classical style of Ottoman architecture. Notably, Gazi Husrev-bey Mosque from 1532 is the largest mosque in Bosnia and Herzegovina, reflecting the early classical school of architecture. Mausoleums and stone tombstones were prevalent as funerary structures, exhibiting various forms that signified the gender and social status of the deceased. The architectural design of *bezistans* ('marketplaces') and *hamams* ('Turkish baths') drew inspiration from the Brusan style, with thermal baths serving as models for private bathrooms. *Madrasas* ('Islamic schools') and *caravanserais* ('inns') incorporated the Hellenistic inner courtyard principle. Residential zones comprised of *mahalas*,

008 D

1

Ottoman-style *Sebilj* on Baščaršija Square by architect Alexander Wittek (1913)

with each featuring 30 to 40 houses, a mosque, a primary school, a *mekteb* ('religious school'), a bakery, and drinking fountains. Traditional Turkish houses with elements such as fences, gardens, and pavilions were prevalent, typically consisting of a stone ground floor for winter housing and a wooden upper floor with a mud-brick filling, opening onto a garden.

During the European influences period (1878–1918) under Austro-Hungarian rule, Sarajevo underwent urban planning and restructuring. The development occurred in three stages. The first involved reorganising the inner city's territory inherited from the Ottoman period, with significant public and administrative buildings located in the western borders. The second stage was partially realised, covering the area from Marindvor to the Military camp. The third stage introduced Novo Sarajevo, featuring an orthogonal base plan with diagonal moves and an emphasis on a rectangular square. The architecture during this period documented the southern concentration of European architectural styles prevalent at the turn of the century within the former Austro-Hungarian monarchy. Eclecticism and Secession dominated, with some works showcasing early elements of modern architecture. Neo-Renaissance public buildings became prominent, while thematic stylistic expressions existed alongside the so-called 'Moorish' architecture, which aimed to generalise oriental building heritage. Secessionist architecture incorporated elements of contemporary architecture and showcased influences from Vienna Secession and art nouveau. Towards the end of the Austro-Hungarian period, modern architecture began emerging and continued into the 1920s and 1930s, marking a shift in architectural thought.

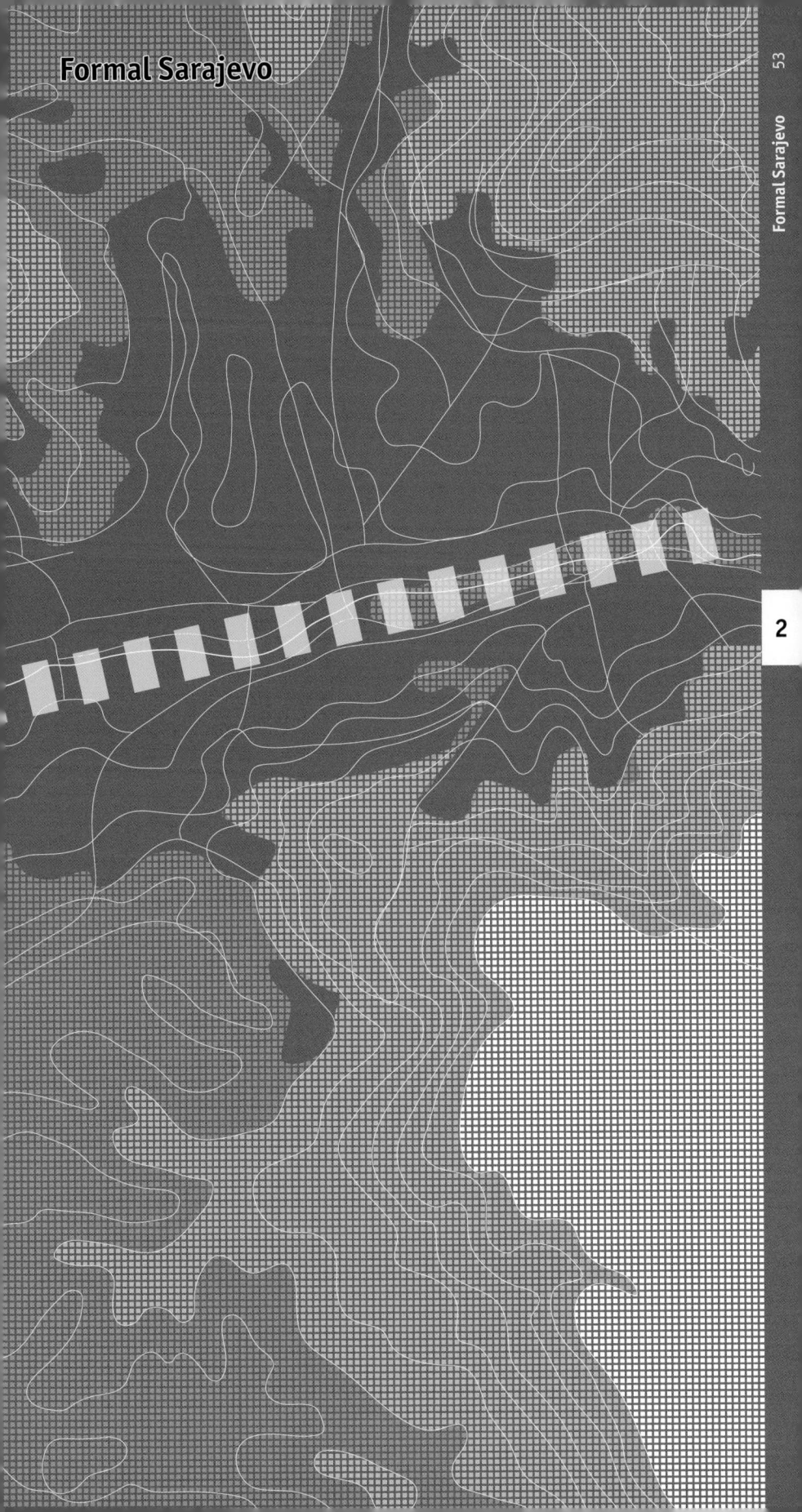

2

View towards the east along the Miljacka River

Formal Sarajevo
Follow the Straight Line

Formal Sarajevo follows the common understanding of the city as a linear configuration along the central axis of Sarajevo valley with its lowest altitude at around 550 m above sea level. It runs along the Miljacka River and the main street, which changes its cross section towards the historical centre from a wide boulevard to a two-lane road. This axis forms the first visual experience of Sarajevo when arriving from the airport and going towards the Old Town. Formal Sarajevo is where one finds most of the free-standing, large-scale, modern / contemporary buildings.

The city's Miljacka River was urbanised through a few phases, starting with the east part of the city and Vijećnica (City Hall). Built in 1896, its flow is completely bounded with the main street and tram line until Skenderija Cultural and Sports Centre, an iconic modernist Sarajevo landmark from 1969 and a transitional area between the historic and modernistic centre of Sarajevo. Further towards the west, the Miljacka flows along the main axis with the exception of the Otoka meander. It is quite natural to follow the river and explore the city's architecture and its distinct historical layers.

The build-up of the longitudinal flow of the city continued intensely during the Socialist Federative Republic of Yugoslavia, with its second contemporary urbanisation after the Austro-Hungarian city development from the Historical Sarajevo chapter.

Formal Sarajevo starts with JAT tower, the city centre's first high-rise by Reuf Kadić, who was among the first architects to introduce modern architecture to Sarajevo. The chapter further explores projects along Titova and Obala Kulina Bana streets, including a national monument of Bosnia and Herzegovina: the Building of the Pension Fund – a curved, corner modernist mixed-use project by Kadić. Many of the projects in this chapter are in the Marijin Dvor neighbourhood, an important cultural and political playground, often referred to as an example of 'unfinished modernisation'. An array of cultural, administrative, office, and hospitality projects lie along its main axis: the Hotel Holiday Inn, the Historical Museum of Bosnia and Herzegovina, Unitic Towers, and one of the distinct works of Juraj Neidhardt – the building of the Parliamentary Assembly.

The RTV Building lies further west from Marijin Dvor, strongly emphasising the Sarajevo axis. A 300-metre-long concrete monolith with a tower was built to be the country's first television facility.

The chapter concludes with large residential urban settlements: Alipašino Polje, with 8,250 units organised in three districts and elliptical urban sequences, and the Dobrinja I and Dobrinja II Olympic Villages, which had clear intentions in the design process to transform the buildings from temporary athlete housing to permanent residences after the Olympics.

Many projects in the Formal Sarajevo chapter were built in the socialist era and then rebuilt after the war in the 1990s. Taking a tram ride along the west-east axis will provide a view of most of the buildings covered in this chapter. Alternatively, the journey is 40 minutes by car in the same direction.

JAT Tower

Ferhadija 2
Reuf Kadić
1947

Vedad Krkbešević

The first high-rise to adorn the city centre and a building with a troubled history still marks the main meeting place and the best viewpoint toward both the older and newer parts of Sarajevo. Designed by the prolific architect of the modernist era, Reuf Kadic, the building was erected atop an old Muslim cemetery and a demolished mosque. The original owner and investor was the Waqf Directorate of the Islamic Community in Bosnia and Herzegovina (inalienable endowment for charity), but the majority of Sarajevans know it as the JAT Tower (Jugoslavenski aerotransport; Jugolavian Air Transport company). Based on the available documentation from before the beginning of the Second World War, we can see that the building was envisioned differently – leaning on the classical Corbusian shapes, with vertical and horizontal windows with black frames as accents on the white plaster background. The top four floors are now inhabited by a renowned hotel with a cafe terrace on all four sides, but the lower part of the 12-storey building is occupied by residents in carefully designed apartments providing ideal views to the surrounding streets.

Irhana Šehović

UPI (Energoinvest) Office Building

010 D

Branilaca Sarajeva 20
Živorad Janković
1962

The UPI building, designed by architect Živorad Janković, is positioned within the urbanistic complex of this city area previously designed by Juraj Neidhardt. The narrow north-south oriented plot has a volumetric composition consisting of a five-storey base with horizontal tendencies and a 12-storey tower in simple cubic form. On the western façade of the building, it is possible to observe the roof of the Grand Synagogue (now the Bosnian Cultural Centre), emphasising the subtle integration of this structure.

The lower volume extends towards the shore, delicately lowering the scale of the building to harmonise with the existing structures mostly built in the Austro-Hungarian era. Although the initial idea included the expansion of Susan Sontag Square to the ground floor of this building to accommodate public facilities, a portion of the square is currently occupied by public city parking, hindering the full realisation of the initial concept. The envelope of the upper volume is materialised in glass in line with the function of the building, while the lower volume features accentuated horizontal lines materialised in stone that penetrate and connect the entire composition, harmonising well with the surrounding existing structures.

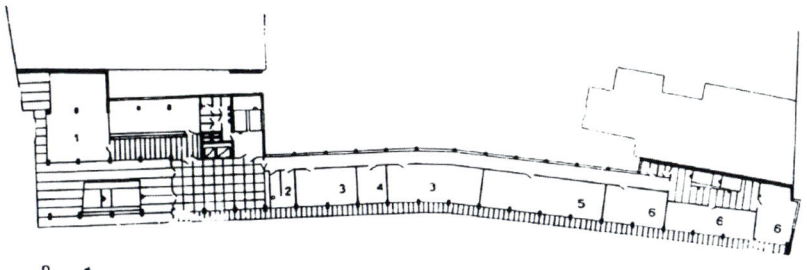

Drawing: Časopis ARH

Philipp Meuser

Šipad Office Building

Maršala Tita 12
Tihomir Ivanović
1956

011 D

The Šipad building occupies a unique position in the city centre at the junction where the main pedestrian street, Titova Street, widens towards Veliki Park. Being a corner building, it starts with a skyscraper on the western side and incorporates elements of central European architecture from the nineteenth century on the eastern side. This design transitions from a vertical to a horizontal setting in terms of its volume. The main façade of the building can be seen as an interpretation of the Austro-Hungarian-period architecture on the opposite side of the street, characterised by pilasters and a vertical configuration. In contrast to the prominently repeated vertical lines, the top floor emphasises the horizontal line that aligns with the street. One distinguishing feature of the building is its recessed ground floor, which creates a 5-metre-wide promenade defined by a colonnade of 'V' columns facing the main street. This design choice facilitates the transition between the narrow sidewalk of Titova Street and the small square adjacent to Veliki Park, providing a pleasant pedestrian experience. Given Sarajevo's climate and the commercial value of street-level spaces, this spatial arrangement proves to be highly advantageous. The Šipad building strives to harmonise with the surrounding urban fabric while incorporating architectural elements that reflect technological progress and the emergence of modernity. The result is a generous public space that could serve as a role model for Sarajevo.

Pasha Oko

Central Bank of Bosnia and Herzegovina

Maršala Tita 25
Milan Zloković
1929–1932

012 D

An architectural competition was held in 1929 for the building that would house the main branch of the Mortgage Bank of the Kingdom of Yugoslavia in Sarajevo. The winning design faced significant criticism, with claims that it did not fit the surrounding area and that its façades did not match one another. As a result, the design was modified, incorporating elements of neoclassical architecture on the front façade, as it was widely believed that bank buildings should include classical elements. The building has a rectangular shape and is constructed entirely of reinforced concrete. The doors and windows are made of oak wood, adorned with various masonry and mosaic decorations. The main street façade is symmetrical and covered in elegant stone slabs, featuring a central entrance point flanked by three large windows on each side. This harmonious rhythm is consistently maintained on the subsequent floors, with windows replacing the entrance door and a stone overhang on the second floor. The stone slabs of the façade extend to the eastern and western façades, after which the final decoration is done in plaster. The initial simplified design without classical

elements remained unchanged. Vladimir Pavlovič Zagorodnjuk designed the intricate decorations and statues that beautifully adorn the building's façade. The two monumental figures of a man and a woman standing at the entrance, gracefully holding lanterns above their heads, draw inspiration from classical Greek art as well as cubism. They artfully incorporate numerous symbols of unity among the people, which were important aspects of society during the time of construction.

2

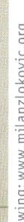

Drawing: www.milanzlokovic.org

Pasha Oko

Studio ZEC

Čobanija Residential Building · 013 D

Čobanija 1
Studio ZEC
2021

This project was created in a context where Sarajevo, as the country's capital and a popular tourist destination, is under heavy pressure from private housing investment. Čobanija Street is unique as it is inextricably linked to the bridge and is close to important public buildings from the Austro-Hungarian period, such as the National Theatre and the Post Office. Although the existing buildings have no architectural significance, the street is important for experiencing the city centre. Another interesting fact is that the street has been flooded with fast-food restaurants over the last 15 years. The fact that the existing and nearby buildings have fewer storeys than the area average had a significant impact on the project. The authors also point out that in such a space, which has the factual value of architecture, it is a kind of 'palimpsest – eternal writing over the written, the text on the text'. The

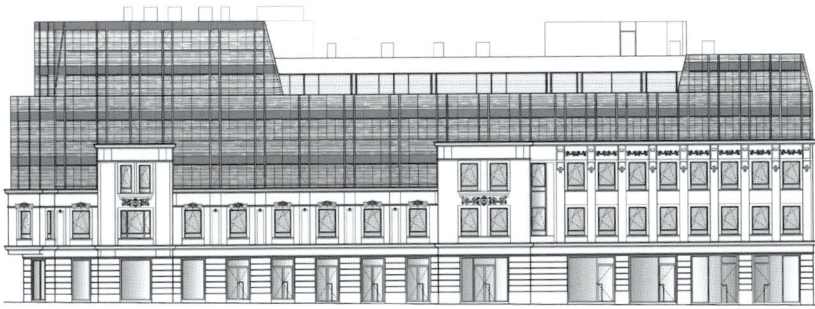

project starts by repeating the front of the old building on Čobanija Street from the east and part of the north and south sides. This keeps the memory of the place alive and makes a 'base' for the building to continue with more floors above. A ground extension of the 'base' of the building is added on the north side towards the river and the main street, completing the whole and emphasising the urban character. Although the horizontal strips make the façades appear neoclassical, they are clearly interrupted by large contemporary openings rotated towards the west side. The upper addition to the building's base is marked by variable floors and a geometry that invokes a roof or mansard, with four additional floors overlooking the main street and the National Theatre or two floors overlooking the south side and Mt. Trebević. Even though this extension adds more space to the building as a whole, the use of perforated metals in front of the glass façades makes the new addition look much lighter and demonstrates a level of contemporary sensitivity to the location.

2

Photos: Anida Krečo

Aria Centre (BBI Centre)

Trg djece Sarajeva 1
Sead Gološ (Grupa Arh)
2009

014 D

Aria (formerly BBI Centre) is a multifunctional complex that occupies the site of the former Sarajka shopping centre, which was severely damaged during the Bosnian War. The complex was designed by Sead Gološ (Grupa Arh), whose designs are characterised by somehow bulky volumes, fragmented façades, and a bold approach to materialisation. And while Sarajka, a symbol of Yugoslav Sarajevo, was sculptural in its form and occupied a central position on the plot, Gološ took a different approach for Aria. The new building is pushed back towards the existing neighbourhood, creating a spacious new town plaza between the building's main façade and a large park to the north. This plaza fast became the primary meeting spot for Sarajevans and serves as an urban anchor for the city centre. Aria's design responds to the plaza with a transparent ground floor, creating an unobstructed inside-outside visual relationship. The structure is divided into two main elements: a horizontal volume with a commercial function and a 10-storey office tower to the northwest. The overlap of these volumes creates a five-storey atrium space connecting the functional elements. The building's façade features contrasting warm and cold materials, including grey aluminium and wood-imitation panels, with glass used as a neutral background element.

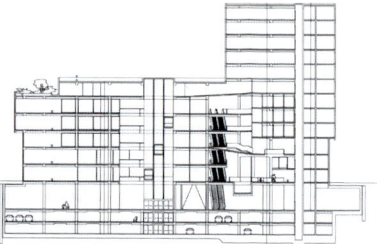

Philipp Meuser

Foreign Trade Chamber of Bosnia and Herzegovina (Kino Dubrovnik)

015 D

Trg djece Sarajeva nn
Milivoj Peterčić
1962

This building designed by Milivoj Peterčić follows the pedestrian path that connects Titova and Mis Irbina streets. It was constructed to house the various cinema halls and office spaces on upper floors. The building is characterised by a clear horizontal tendency, emphasised by alternating solid lines materialised in the light texture of stone in contrast to negative glass openings. The structure deliberately interacts with the nearby square through a recessed ground floor, a passage through the centre of the building, and a prominently accented horizontal roof above the entrance to the former cinema where the cinema terrace is located. The building has several entrances, the main one being through the passage, with additional entrances along the building's periphery. The façade of this four-storey office building is dominated by office spaces with an eastern orientation, while the recessed top floor stands out as a representative feature of the architecture of that time. Built at the same time as the UPI (Energoinvest) Office Building, which is adjacent to the Grand Synagogue and National Theatre, this building exemplifies a significant urban infill that integrates into the block urban matrix and creates a contemporary ambiance in central Sarajevo.

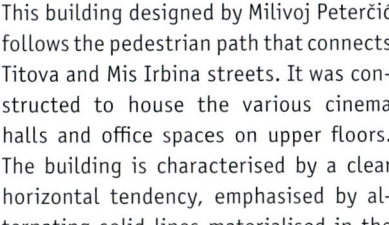

2

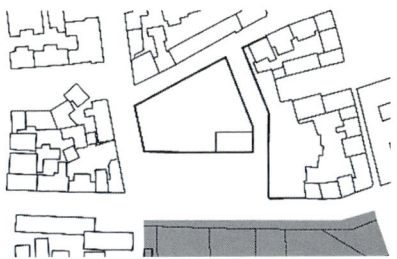

Festina Lente Bridge

016 D

Obala Maka Dizdara 3
Alagić Adnan, Hrustić Amila,
Kanlić Bojan
2012

Throughout history, Sarajevo's city centre developed around the Miljacka River, which became adorned with numerous bridges. This bridge is the youngest after the Ars Aevi Bridge. It is positioned in a very sensitive location where it was needed for a long time. It connects Radićeva Street, an inviting pedestrian area, to the Academy of Fine Arts – the famous building designed by architect Karel Paržik in 1899 as an Evangelical Church. Festina Lente, meaning 'hurry up slowly', was the winning project at the public competition in 2007. It was submitted by three second-year students at the Academy of Fine Arts. The 38-metre-long and 4- to 7-metre-wide bridge is made of a steel structure covered with aluminium plates, with two wooden benches under the central loop. Although the construction was very demanding because its form violated

Dženat Dreković

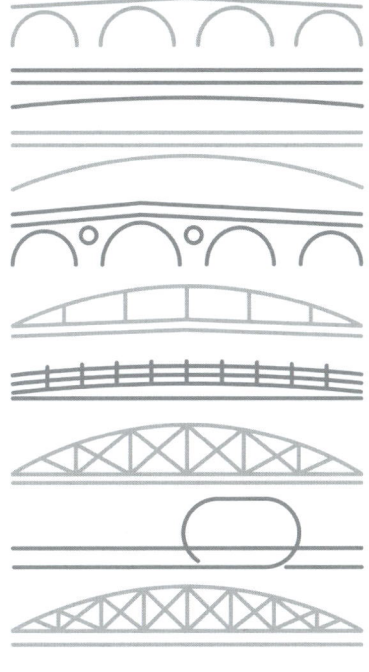

Illustration: Molimao, Sandin Mededović

standard static principles, which led to certain adjustments, over the years it improved the quality of Sarajevo's public space, aiming to become one of the city's contemporary symbols.

Academy of Performing Arts  017 D

Skenderija nn
Jonus Ademović (author),
Zvjezdan Turkić, AKSA (local
architect of record)
2008–2023

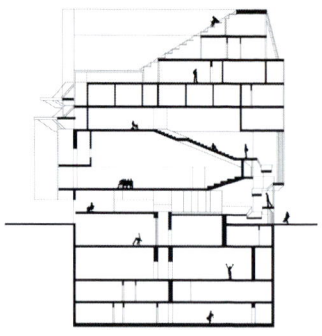

The Academy of Performing Arts is one of the rare examples of a contemporary public and educational building constructed after the 1990s in Sarajevo. The project was chosen from among the entries in a 2008 international competition that attracted numerous architects. The competition brief suggested a 5,500-square-metre dense programme for the constrained plot next to the Skenderija Cultural and Sports Centre, leaning on an existing Austro-Hungarian residential building on its western side. The author viewed the competition brief's traditional programmatic departmental division as 'inadequate and contrary to the interdisciplinary way of artistic production'. The programme is instead divided into areas with natural light and dark zones, while the in-between grey zone includes the 'Big Stage' in the central part of the building. Avoiding the black-box effect in the above-ground levels was made possible by placing the dark areas in the basement. It is interesting to notice the contemporary approach of opening the school to the public by creating carved-in public and semi-public zones, starting from the small entrance square to the vestibule, through visually open ramps, towards the Main Stage, then passing by the Small Stage up to the roof programmed for an open-air cinema stage looking directly towards Mt. Trebević. Depending on the orientation and surroundings, the Corten and glazed façade components overlap on each side. From the fully Corten façade on the south to the glazed north street façade with a system of ramps and the upper administrative zone, the eastern entrance façade serves as a visual transition marked by cascading Corten that suggests movement towards the roof stage. Although the building's construction began in 2010, a number of administrative and financial issues caused the project to remain unfinished for many years.

Timur Babić

Nihad Babović

2

Delegation of the European Union and German Embassy

018 D

Skenderija 3
Nihad Babović
2005–2008

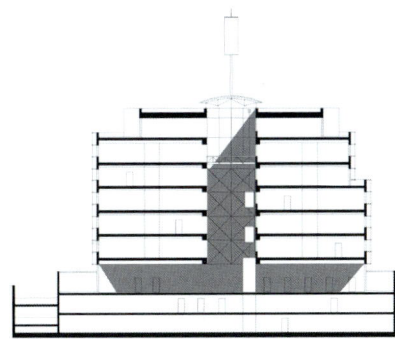

The building of the Delegation of the European Union is in the Skenderija neighbourhood on the left bank of the Miljacka River, close to the city centre zone at the transition where the residential zone ends. The building also houses the German Embassy. It has a total area of 13,000 m², of which 6,000 m² are below ground. The nine-storey structure has two technical floors with parking below, a ground floor that serves as the main entrance and has public amenities, and six levels of office space above. The structure is made up of two parallel office buildings connected by a glazed atrium street and has gardens on both sides, while the design was determined by high-level safety and security requirements. The street sides lack office windows, and a high stone-lined wall surrounds the garden and yard, forming an architectural coherence with the building. The author's objective was to create a contemporary interpretation of a palace typology as well as use features from Bosnian traditional architecture. As a reference to the window iron grills of historic Sarajevo buildings, a unique system of double façades with glass panels enclosed in a stainless-steel structure was created. The roof between the buildings, the glass façades, the glass on stainless steel frames, and the stone façade all contribute to the building's main architectural expression. On the ground floor, after all of the security checks, there is a public area. The ground floor has meeting and lecture halls, as well as a street, café, press conference space, a fountain, and a small square. Office spaces are on the upper levels, which are accessible through panoramic elevators in two slats. A bridge connects the slats solely on a single level.

Irhana Šehović

Gymnasium Obala

Obala Kulina bana 3
Muhamed Kadić, 1946
Karel Pařík, 1906

019 D

Obala Gymnasium is a representative of the late Austro-Hungarian period. While the first two parts of this period focused on mimicking Viennese architecture and developing neo-styles, in the later one we can see tendencies to intermix the local and historical context with the principles of Western European urbanism. The building was initially designed by architect Karel Paržik, and later adapted by Muhamed Kadić in 1946. Unlike typical Austro-Hungarian façades, Obala Gymnasium features a retracted central part creating an open courtyard. This outlines the entrance sequence as a gesture for the building typology, but also creates a strong reference to the Ottoman buildings organised around an inner courtyard.

The original building was done in a restrained classicist manner, with almost no ornaments on the side façades and with large, accentuated openings towards the river. By leaving behind the busy street and walking through a calm green space, one enters the building in its centre between two wings with classrooms. This middle block was destroyed during the Second World War. However, soon after, there was a heightened need for a gymnasium and great efforts were made to return its function to the centre of Sarajevo. The entrance façade was made light and a covered porch resting on pillars was added. The new middle block referenced the existing wings using the height of the cornice and to some extent the division of the openings. On both sides, where the new central block connects to the wings, the perforated vertical elements clearly show the sensitivity towards the inherited composition of the original design.

City of Sarajevo and Parliament of the Federation of Bosnia and Herzegovina

020 D

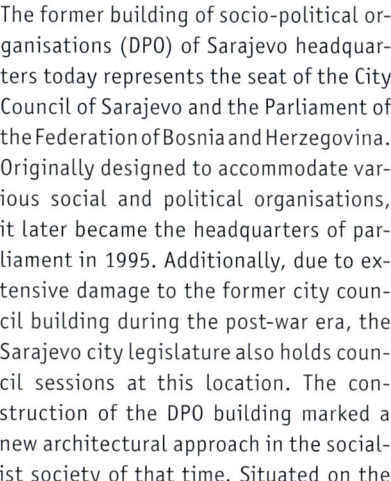

Hamdije Kreševljakovića 3
Vladimir Dobrović
1980

The former building of socio-political organisations (DPO) of Sarajevo headquarters today represents the seat of the City Council of Sarajevo and the Parliament of the Federation of Bosnia and Herzegovina. Originally designed to accommodate various social and political organisations, it later became the headquarters of parliament in 1995. Additionally, due to extensive damage to the former city council building during the post-war era, the Sarajevo city legislature also holds council sessions at this location. The construction of the DPO building marked a new architectural approach in the socialist society of that time. Situated on the left bank of the Miljacka River, its exterior features a predominantly stone façade complemented by sections covered with aluminium tin and reflective glass surfaces. The contrasting elements of white stone, black aluminium tin, and gleaming mirrored glass give the building a distinct visual appeal. The entrance square notably stands out with a hovering two-storey cube positioned diagonally from the main body and the river axis, gracefully connecting the building to the recreational zone of Obala Maka Dizdara. The main structure comprises five storeys, with a uniform façade facing the adjacent building on Obala Maka Dizdara on one side and culminating in a mansard roof adjacent to the entrance square. Despite its altered function following the war in the 1990s, the building underwent reconstruction while preserving its original form and materials, maintaining its contribution to the quality of public space.

Stjepan Anzulović

Pension Fund Building

022 D

Hamze Hume
Muhamed Kadić, Reuf Kadić
1940–1942

The Kadić brothers, the architects of several of the most notable pre-war modern architecture achievements in Sarajevo and Bosnia and Herzegovina, created a modernist retail, office, and residential building on the corner of one of the busiest intersections in the city, at Maršal Tito and Hamza Humo streets. Long before the intersection was built, the location was considered complex because it represented a symbolic gap between several landmarks from various historical eras, posing a particularly delicate task. Some of the architectural language used in other designs by the Kadić brothers is repeated in the building: glazed corners, this time arced to follow the shape of the building, rows of large windows, cantilevered upper floors, ceramic tiles, and roof terraces. The main façade curves at

Irhana Šehović

Rapid Office Building

021 D

Valtera Perića 10
Bogdan Stojkov
1960s

Situated at the intersection of Valtera Perica, Hiseta, and Hamze Hume streets, this building occupies a unique location, with blocks from the Austro-Hungarian period on one side and one of the city's major intersections on the other. The structure itself is designed to complete the block formation between the two streets. Its base follows the trapezoid shape of the plot up to three storeys, then transitions into an eight-storey tower facing the east side. The building concludes with a recessed top floor, topped with a slender slab. While the building's two lateral façades lean inward, the main façade slightly leans outward, showcasing the sensitivity associated with the intersection of the two diagonal streets. A repeated glazing strip and continuous horizontal line run through all sides of the building, altering the perception of scale and enhancing the openness of the surrounding public space.

Amer Kapetanović

the corner, with repetitive large windows and loggias facing east, while the cantilevered first floor along Hamze Hume Street repeats the curvature and connects to the vertical plane of the northern side. The combination of two distinct but complementary façades results in a distinctive yet sensitive form that blends the building into its surroundings. In 2008, this building was officially declared a protected national monument of Bosnia and Herzegovina.

2

Amer Kapetanović

Federal Health Institute

023 D

Maršala Tita 9

Tihomir Ivanović

1952

Red Cross Building ↘

024 C

Kranjčevićeva 2

Helen Baldasar

1928–1929

This is one of the significant public service buildings in Sarajevo that was constructed in the years following the conclusion of the Second World War. It is located at the largest intersection in the central business district of the city where Maal Tito Street and Alipaina Street meet. This structure is now home to a number of government agencies, including the National Agency for Medicines and Food as well as the Federal Health Institute. The central four floors of the southern façade are set back from the main structure body. These floors are dominated by parallel pillars that stretch from the first floor all the way up to the ceiling level of the third floor. These pillars highlight the cubic façade, which is completely coated with marble stone. The building's main entrance is situated in the middle and it is framed by a one-storey-high canopy featuring square perforations on each side. Its identical window rows on each floor reflect the time period in which it was built, while the scale and repetition of the pillars complement the wide, busy urban street.

Due to the building's status as one of the city's earliest examples of modern architecture, it was given the status of a national monument. Offices, a public kitchen and bath, and a cinema were some of the uses that the building served over the years. The structure was shelled during the war in the 1990s, and it was later completely destroyed in a fire. However, it was reconstructed in 2018. As a protected national monument, the regulations for the reconstruction were extremely stringent. The building had to be brought back to its initial design, or as close as possible to it. This was accomplished, for the most part, and the building was reconstructed to its symmetrical, cubical form, consisting of one central part and two side parts. The building's primary access point is located in the central portion directly below a slender balcony with rounded edges, and there are two additional entrances on either side of it. The double-height vertical lines that frame the windows and rise above the volume divide the building's main horizontality in the central entry part.

Rabbit Wolf

Union Bank Building (Jugobanka)

025 D

Dubrovačka 6
Zdravko Kovačević, Milan Kušan
1966

Developed as a cultural and business centre for the Yugoslavian Foreign Trade Bank headquarters in Sarajevo, this project was nominated by Bosnia and Herzegovina for the 1966 Borba Award, a prestigious annual award for the best urban-architectural realisation in Yugoslavia awarded by *Borba* magazine in cooperation with the Association of Architects of Yugoslavia. As part of the nation's modernisation process, the bank was restructured and renamed Jugobanka. The five-storey building parallel to the street is completely glazed, and the top is stepped back, covered with an overhanging flat roof framed by a stone frieze. The lower orthogonal protruding volume appears cantilevered towards the southern Mali Park and pedestrian area, while on the other side, it is tucked beneath the main volume, forming an accentuated, long covered entrance on an elevated ground floor. Along with the entry steps and amphitheatre volume, the recognisable detached roof plane appears to be floating in the park.

2

Rabbit Wolf

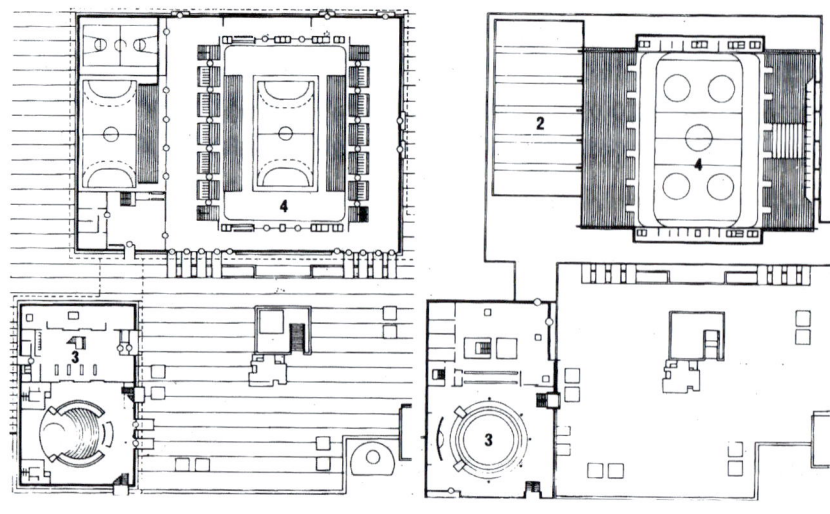

Cultural and Sports Centre Skenderija (Mirza Delibašić)

026 D

Terezija bb
Živorad Janković, Halid Muhasilović, Ognjeslav Malkin
1969

The Cultural and Sports Centre Skenderija, an iconic landmark of Sarajevo, made its opening debut in 1969 with the premiere screening of *Bitka na Neretvi* ('Battle of Neretva'), attended by Sarajevans and the then President of the Socialist Federative Republic of Yugoslavia, Josip Broz Tito. The same year, it was awarded the Borba Award, a prestigious annual award for the best urban-architectural realisation in Yugoslavia awarded by *Borba* magazine in cooperation with the Association of Architects of Yugoslavia. Comprising three buildings arranged around a large plateau (the Main Hall, the Ice Hall, and the Youth Hall), Skenderija also boasts a commercial centre located under the plateau that provides a covered connection to all the parts. In the following years, this combination of programmes served as a model for similar complexes throughout Yugoslavia. The buildings' exteriors are a testament to

Archive

the concept of honest representation of the constructive system, featuring large spans and simple concrete and glass façades. The simplicity of the structure is expressed through the openness of the constructive system in raw concrete. Skenderija's significance is not limited to its avant-garde architecture; it also facilitated the expansion of the city centre towards the west and south, opening up the southern bank of the Miljacka and the slopes of Trebević to the city. The complex's scale allowed for cultural, political, artistic, social, economic, and sporting events that could rival those of larger cities such as Belgrade and Zagreb, giving Sarajevo new-found cultural significance. This was further cemented by the Winter Olympics held in the city in 1984. Even today, the centre serves its original purpose; while only two halls are in use, the rest of the complex houses shops and cafés. In 2017, the government considered selling the complex to foreign developers, which would have led to the demolition of the original buildings to prepare the site for a new development. Local civic organisations expressed their disapproval, and the project has been put on hold.

2

Philipp Meuser

The Marijin Dvor area: Central business and commercial district with some of the most representative contemporary buildings in Sarajevo

Steven Anzulović

Anida Krečo

Dvor Residential Building

Hiseta 10
AHAKNAP (Adnan Harambašić, Kenan Brčkalija)
2013

The Dvor housing project found its spot as part of the emerging Marijin Dvor commercial and cultural centre. Starting its development in the nineteenth century, this part of the city's urban tissue is organised in apartment blocks with wide orthogonal streets. Following the new plan for redevelopment, the same organisation principle continued and Dvor made up the first corner of the future block. The adjacent Austro-Hungarian apartment buildings are an important contextual element. Dvor has 42 living units distributed across six floors and a commercial ground floor. The primary orientation for the project, which was set by the new urban plan, is predominantly north. This demanding orientation became the cornerstone for the project and its formative expression. The body of the building is partially rotated, and as a result, part of every apartment comes out towards the south/west to introduce light into the interior. The sculptural expression is balanced by a grid of regularly spaced windows with bright red frames, giving the building a contemporary expression. This colour together with the distinct window fences creates references to Bosnian modernism. The project is finished off with a semi-public rooftop terrace – a sensible yet rare element in new housing developments in Sarajevo. With an evident Scandinavian influence, the rooftop visually and spatially connects the building and its users with the natural and built landscape rising around the building.

Anida Krečo

Embassy and Apartments FAR

Maglajska 4
Nihad Babović / hmd architects
2016

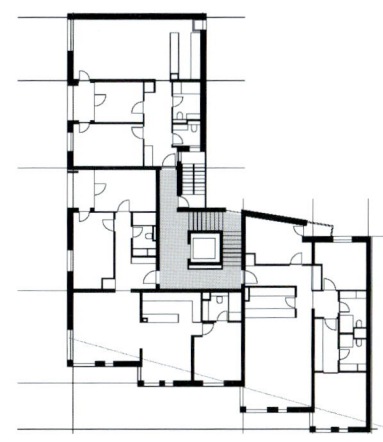

The building is situated along Hiseta, the main city street from Marijin Dvor to Skenderija, forming a block with the Dvor residential building. The Embassy of the Republic of Slovenia occupies the ground and first floors, which are formally separate from the residential portion of the building on the upper levels, with two retracted top floors with penthouses and terraces. The embassy has three entrances: the main entrance, the consular entrance, and the public access to the passage where an exhibition and meeting hall are located. The entrance to the residential part of the building on the other side is through the building's porch. The architects sought to make contemporary parallels to historic architecture. Apart from massive stone plinths and travertine cladding, the most distinctive elements project towards the main street – an allusion to traditional *doksat*. The result is an appropriate urban appearance for this zone, as well as a quality highlight for all the apartments – the unique views of the Miljacka River and bridges extending all the way to the old town and the At Mejdan Park. The public space beneath these cantilevers, directly adjacent to the tram line, forms part of Sarajevo's main axis' increasingly frequent pedestrian communication.

Nihad Babović

2

Nihad Babović

Nihad Babović

GrupaArh Archive

Bau-Herc Residential and Office Building

Maglajska 1
Sead Gološ (Grupa Arh)
2019

029 C

The Bau-Herc residential and office building is located in the central Marijin Dvor neighbourhood of Sarajevo that dates back to the Austro-Hungarian period of the city's development. Bau-Herc, or the 'rusty building' as the citizens of Sarajevo commonly refer to it, is a five-storey building with an underground garage that hosts IT companies over two middle floors, a ground floor coffee shop and restaurant, and a residential floor at its very top that comes out to the rooftop terrace overlooking the city. Its corner position enabled the formation of a small public plaza that continues on to the

pedestrian area of Vilsonovo šetalište to the west. There were several façade proposals when the project was introduced to the public in 2018. One included shining white aluminium plates, but after rather negative backsplash from the public, the architect decided to use perforated Corten plates to try to tone down and interpolate the new building into the historic neighbourhood.

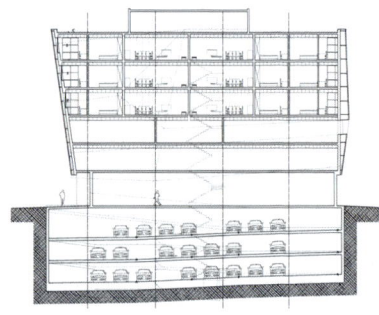

GrupaArh Archive

029

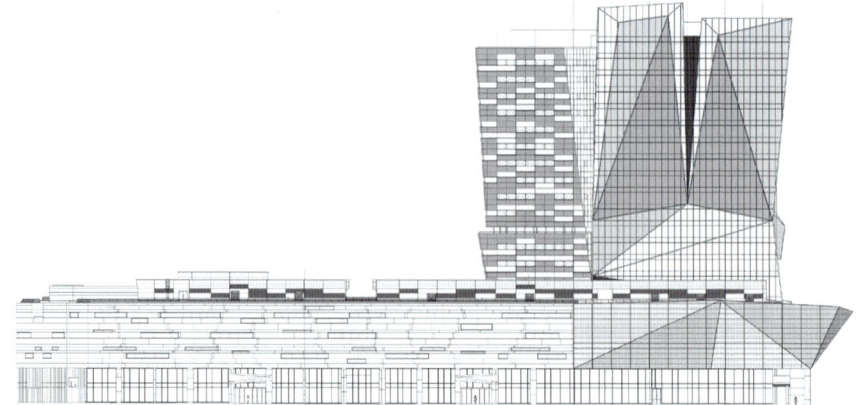

Sarajevo City Centre

Vrbanja 1
Sead Gološ (Grupa Arh)
2014

030 **C**

The multifunctional Sarajevo City Centre is located in the Marijin Dvor central business district. It consists of four separate parts: a five-star hotel, commercial and office space, a shopping centre, and an underground garage. The largest part of the building is the shopping centre. On an area measuring 49,000 square metres, there are more than 180 shops dedicated to fashion, sports, technology, and entertainment, making it the busiest and biggest shopping centre in a city in Bosnia and Herzegovina. The two adjacent office and hotel towers are merged into a singular structure, visually differentiated by the materialisation of their façades: steel and glass. Although the general public opinion on this building varies, its scale and dynamic form have shaped it into one of the city's most recognisable landmarks.

Philipp Meuser

Philipp Meuser

Parliamentary Assembly of Bosnia and Herzegovina

Trg Bosne i Hercegovine 1
Juraj Neidhardt
1982

031 **C**

In 1955, Juraj Neidhardt won a national design competition for proposals on a new master plan for Marijin Dvor, including a new Parliamentary Assembly building. His interpretation of the Ottoman legacy was clearly indicated in both in his urban proposal and the new building design. Neidhardt wanted to make sure that the Bosnian Oriental influence did not remain confined only to historical Sarajevo, but rather integrated into the new city fabric. The proposal included cultural and administrative buildings in a seemingly free urban disposition. Relating the site to a greater city area, the proposal aimed at easing traffic on the main axis by introducing two new transversals and a pedestrian diagonal connecting the Parliamentary Assembly site with the railway station on one side and Mt. Trebević on the other, presenting Marijin Dvor as a demarcation between the old and new city. Following the competition, realisation of the winning proposal was postponed. The master plan was only partially executed, and the administrative ensemble completed three decades later,

becoming the headquarters for all republic institutions. The ensemble comprises a four-storey elongated volume with a contrasting tower, tied together with a public plaza. The elongated volume was formed parallel to the axis and offset in order to introduce the new plaza towards the north for approximately 100,000 visitors. Neidhardt proposed the new skyscraper as an accent as well as an orientation point for the wider Sarajevo region, referring to all other parliaments and their towers as a specific typology. With its height, the assembly responds to the National Museum further west, while the executive council tower directly relates to the tall buildings on its east side. The spatial arrangement of the volumes as well as their elevations were based on symbolic predecessors; a tower / clock-tower, an atrium, pillar hall / triem, and in an initial proposal, a cupola-covered shared space. Neidhardt suggested that the horizontal volume took inspiration in the elongated

ANUBIH

Faculty of Philosophy

Franje Račkog 1
Juraj Neidhardt
1955–1959

032 **C**

This three-storey building visually aligns with the height of the existing National Museum on one side, while on the other side, it withdraws volumetrically to achieve a better visual perception of the Parliament of Bosnia and Herzegovina. In its rectangular Z-shaped floor plan, it forms two courtyards, one of which is a green antechamber leading to the central open-configured hall with a staircase inclined towards the entrance, serving as a unified entity and a meeting point. The ground floor accommodates the faculty's auditorium, the largest lecture hall, alongside the dean's office, while classrooms for various subjects are located on the upper floors. The building façade is clad in stone, with the ground floor featuring a coarser finish reminiscent of traditional architectural expression, topped by a strong horizontal canopy and connecting element that accentuates the dynamic floor plan configuration. The upper floors of the building are finished in polished stone material, with a repetitive alternation of solid and void panels typical for educational institutions.

bay window (*doksat*), commonly associated with Ottoman domestic architecture. At the time, it was the only building with this purpose designed in a modern style in this part of Europe. Instead of standard large formats and intimidating buildings for the administrative functions, the form of this ensemble is light, with both the interior and exterior pointing to Corbusier's teachings. The dynamic relationship between the volumes was rather emphasised with their convex-concave form, a thin waist on the lower bulky volume, and a slight 'stomach' on the tall elegant one. During the war in the 1990s, located at the front line, the ensemble suffered major damage. The building's interior was refurbished in 2008 and the exterior façade was reconstructed with minor structural changes in 2009.

2

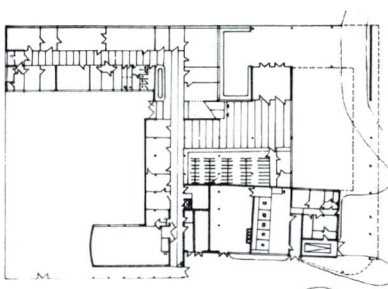

Philipp Meuser

Unitic Towers
(Unis Towers)

Fra Anđela Zvizdovića 1
Ivan Štraus
1986–1987

The 23-storey towers were designed on a plot in the city centre and commissioned by the former Yugoslav business giant UNIS. They were intended to host the administrative and technical departments of the company. The two towers were made identical, developed around a reinforced concrete core, and are connected with a horizontal volume at the ground floor level. This volume houses the main entrance for both towers, along with all the mutual facilities required. With the additional horizontal volume, the whole spans over a total of 40,000 m². It is clad with a reflective glass skin, keeping the exterior as simple as possible. The towers feature several specific reinforced concrete elements, such as the ventilation system, the staircase at the entrance, and two concrete caps on top of each tower. The concrete caps serve as technical and maintenance floors as well as rainwater collectors. They are distinctively shaped, recognisable as the architect's design, and provide a contrasting element to the glass skin of the towers. The caps are also intended and currently used for advertising placements, as the architect wanted to make reference to the BMW Tower in Munich and the Genex Tower in Belgrade. Today, the UNITIC Towers host some of the most important IT companies as well as a number of other businesses and international non-governmental organisations. At the time of their construction, the UNIS Towers did not receive a warm welcome from the general public, as their height and contemporary look did not resonate

with the local community. As a form of acceptance, Sarajevans came up with nicknames for the towers: Momo and Uzeir. Both towers were destroyed and burned down during the Siege of Sarajevo in the 1990s, but they were quickly rebuilt after the war, cementing their place as one of the most iconic and memorable landmarks of Sarajevo.

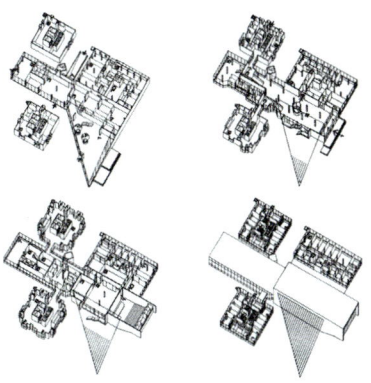

ADS Stduio

Avaz Twist Tower
Tešanjska 24a
Faruk Kapidžić
2008

 034 C

2

Avaz Twist Tower is the tallest structure in Sarajevo and one of the tallest in the region, serving as the headquarters of one of the country's leading newspapers. With a height of 172 metres, including the antenna spire, the tower boasts 40 storeys above ground level and is equipped with seven elevators. Positioned adjacent to the central Marijin Dvor neighbourhood, it is visible from all parts of the city. With its distinctive twisted form, the Avaz Twist Tower bears resemblance to iconic structures such as the Turning Torso in Sweden by Santiago Calatrava and Milan's Generali Tower in Italy by Zaha Hadid Architects. However, the tower's design has been adapted to accommodate the local construction industry.

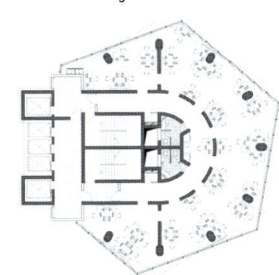

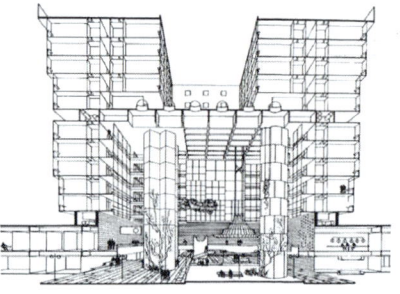

Philipp Meuser

Holiday Inn Hotel

035 C

Zmaja od Bosne 4
Ivan Štraus
1981–1983

The first architectural concept for the Holiday Inn Hotel was initially made in 1969. After rounds of adjustments and refinements, the construction of Sarajevo's splendid Holiday Inn Hotel finally commenced in 1981. The architect behind the project described it as a contemporary interpretation of Morića Han – an inn from the Ottoman period that boasted an enchanting inner garden, providing weary travellers with a place to rest in Sarajevo's Old Town. His vision aimed to evoke an ambiance reminiscent of a covered public plaza, resulting in a lobby that gracefully extended through five of the ten hotel floors. To achieve the illusion of a boundless space, the architect adorned the galleries with reflective glass, which was subsequently replaced with a fence in 1996. In his book *15 Years of Bosnian and Herzegovinian Architecture*, published in 1987, the architect Ivan Štraus drew attention to several parallels between his own design and the works of the renowned American architect John Portman, who was active during the same period. Štraus humorously attributed these similarities to the unique paths and design preferences that intersected at a particular moment in both of their lives. In contrast to Portman's choice of façades, he opted for a vibrant colour palette dominated by shades of yellow, ochre, and brown. These hues followed the upward dynamic of the hotel's façade, while the architect also insisted on referencing the local traditional architecture through interpretation of the *doksat* – a projecting architectural element repeated throughout all of the façades.

Alta Shopping Centre

Franca Lehara 2
Studio Nonstop (Sanja Galić-Grozdanić, Igor Grozdanić)
2005–2010

The Alta shopping centre is strategically situated in the Marijin Dvor central business district at one of the intersections with the most significant pedestrian and vehicular traffic. The impressive structure complements the plot adjacent to the Unitic (Unis) Towers and stands directly across from the Parliamentary Assembly of Bosnia and Herzegovina. Thanks to its enviable location, the architects designed it as an urban shopping gallery, showcasing upscale retail establishments on the basement, ground, and three upper levels. The continuous shopping street gracefully unfolds on all floors around the central void, forming a captivating three-dimensional structure that the architects aptly named the 'Bosnian Knot'. This design concept aims to seamlessly accommodate the dynamic flow of urban pedestrians while harmoniously integrating with the surrounding urban landscape. The building's overall volume follows the primary longitudinal axis, serving to highlight the clarity and coherence of the fundamental concept. Diverging from the conventional shopping mall typology, extensive glazed surfaces imbue an inviting sense of openness towards the city.

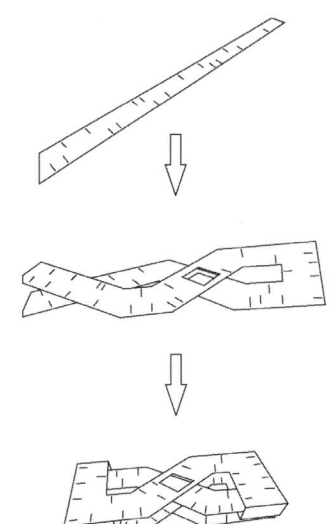

Sandro Lendler

2

Sandro Lendler

Railway Station

037 C

Put života 2
*Bogdan Stojkov, Lorenc
Eichberger, Jahiel Finci,
Muhamed Kadić, Emanuel
Šamanek, Dušan Smiljanić*
1947–1952

At the cross section of the Sarajevo valley between Kovačići and Velešići hills, on a flat area of approximately 1.2 km lies a marker of an idealistic idea from the mid-1950s: Sarajevo Railway Station. Its rail tracks follow the lowest contour of Hum and Velešići from west to north, while the building stretches as a tangent line to it. The central hall and two wings are oriented away from the tracks and use a mirrored curve to emphasise their relationship to one of the largest urban plazas in Sarajevo, which was envisioned to extend over a planned diagonal axis of the city (not realised). It started two years after the Second World War as a visionary goal of physically uniting the country through its railway system. The project was conceived as a public competition won by a group of Czechoslovakian architects. By 1948, a political drift between Yugoslavia and the USSR meant that the architects left the country and the project, which was finished by local architects in 1953. Semi-circular in plan, the volume's disposition is symmetrical. The building's front façade features a rigid grid with emphasised verticals and a grandiose glass skin on the central volume. A sculptural concrete hyperbolic paraboloid roof spans the central area and rises from the tracks towards the city, creating a strong welcoming vista. Sarajevo Railway Station and the square in front were declared a national monument of Bosnia and Herzegovina in 2016. The building's large scale even now far exceeds the city's needs. With fewer than ten trains arriving daily, the station remains mostly empty.

Post Office Building at Railway Station

038 C

Put života nn
Bogdan Stojkov
1950s

The Post Office in the Railway Station in Sarajevo is almost unnoticeable next to the Railway Station building, but at the same time, an experienced observer will not miss it. Its front façade consists of two storeys materialised in a local manner: the stone covered ground floor and an almost floating first storey characterised by framed horizontal windows speak to the era in which it was built. The real complexity of the building can be observed only from a higher viewpoint – this is when the viewer starts to comprehend the true size of this building that is almost 100 metres in length and almost 50 metres wide. Public spaces are designed on the ground floor, while the rest of the building is used for post storage.

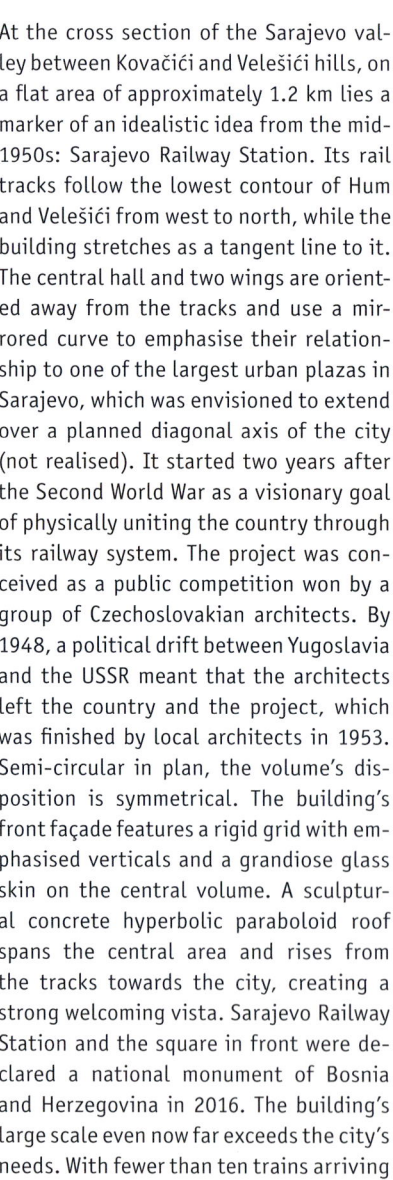

2

Railway Traffic Control and Communication Tower

039 C

Put života 12
Said Jamaković
1982

The tower is made up of distinct volumes, with three vertical tower-like volumes toward the west and the railway tracks and one lower volume facing the street. The author describes the design as 'the intention of supporting the materialisation and stylistic features of the previous buildings and superimposing compatible canons', which could be interpreted as a reference to the station's vertical strips and the post office's sleek volume. In contrast to the others, its façade facing the tracks is entirely covered with glass prisms and a glass screen for traffic controllers. The square-shaped stone cladding and glass prism are repeated throughout all volumes, giving the building a distinct identity.

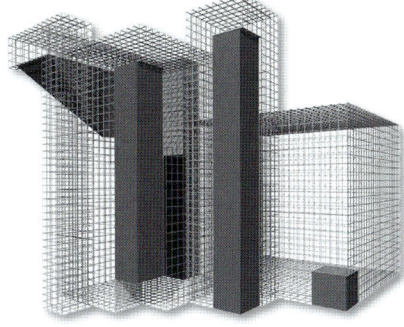

Historical Museum of Bosnia and Herzegovina (Museum of Revolution)

040 C

Zmaja od Bosne 5
*Boris Magaš, Edo Šmidihen,
Radovan Horvat*
1958–1963

The building of the Historical Museum of Bosnia and Herzegovina is located within the historic sensitive urban fabric of Sarajevo's city centre in Marijin Dvor, which has a specific position within the city's linear structure, where it works as a joint – a natural link between the historic centre and the modern city zone, between the old and the new. The idea submitted by the then-young authors Magaš, Šmidihen, and Horvat won first place in a public competition in 1958 and took five years to finish with minimal modifications. A striking enclosed cuboid form measuring 27 × 27 × 5 m hovers on nine steel piers above the glazed entrance and an elongated strip volume of nearly 70 m. The entrance platform stands on a raised stone plinth that conceals the basement and a lowered inner garden. The platform is lined with square slabs of white Brač stone two metres above the street and is therefore clearly perceived as a podium, which is ascended by floating stone steps. By climbing the platform, the visitor is in a certain sense excluded from the public and enters a more private space. In the further access sequence approaching via the stone bridge under the cube, the transparency of the glass façade of the ground floor allows one to see the interior and thus psychologically prepare for new discoveries. Upon entering the lobby, you can see the inner garden, the central staircase leading to the cuboid, and the glazed corridor along the façade that leads to the presentation hall and gallery. A white, stone-clad cuboid highlights the

Sabina Hodović

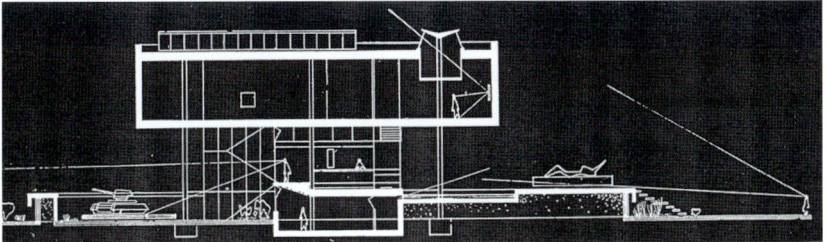

Ivan Štraus Archive

2

monumentality of the building. The elevated main exhibition space is also emphasised by the appearance of a floating volume, which is achieved by its separation from the pedestal by a modular grid of glass surfaces that at the entrance level very subtly connect visitors with the environment. In such a way, its immediate environment gained a clear entrance sequence as an attractive part of the public space and the opposite side as an intimate space of the garden, which brings the museum activities into an active relationship with nature. This museum presents a true architectural showpiece that is in line with European and global movements from the early years of the latter half of the twentieth century.

Ivan Štraus Archive

Ars Aevi Bridge

Marijin Dvor, Vilsonovo šetalište
RPBW, Renzo Piano
2002

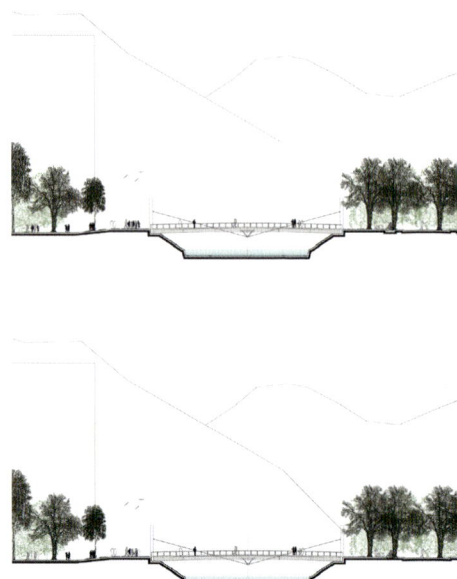

The Ars Aevi Foundation was established during the first months of the siege of Sarajevo from 1992 to 1995, as a utopian activities project in the contemporary arts field and as a cultural and information centre, as well as a virtual museum. It was virtual because the artworks that were donated from various countries for solidarity reasons starting from the first month of the siege were at first stored in their place of origin and only at the end of the war were they brought to Sarajevo and temporarily stored in a warehouse, waiting for a final destination. In 1999, the first exhibition of the entire collection opened in a structure made available by the city. On that occasion, the architect Renzo Piano became involved as a UNESCO Goodwill Ambassador and agreed to design the future museum. On the same occasion, the Mayor of the City and the Canton Ministers selected the area on Marijin Dvor Kvadrant C next to the existing historical museum to be the location for the new museum. The new contemporary art museum thus became an important signal of the will of Sarajevo city to resurge after the material and spiritual devastation. As a sewing element on the river, the project foresaw a pedestrian bridge to connect the residential and cultural area and reach the avenue that is one of the most important communication arterials of the city. The symmetrical discrete structure is composed of two pillars on both sides that mark the entry and support the sleek glued laminated timber beams. Unlike all other Sarajevan stone, metal, and concrete bridges, it generates distinct vibrations when pedestrians cross. In the spirit of this idea, which was to start the project in phases without waiting for finances, Venice-based engineering studio Favero & Milan and other Italian and international companies that provided materials constructed the pedestrian bridge. It instantly improved the public space and circulation in the recreational area and neighbouring residential area, marking yet another milestone in the larger scale project of the Ars Aevi Museum of Contemporary Art.

Ars Aevi Archive

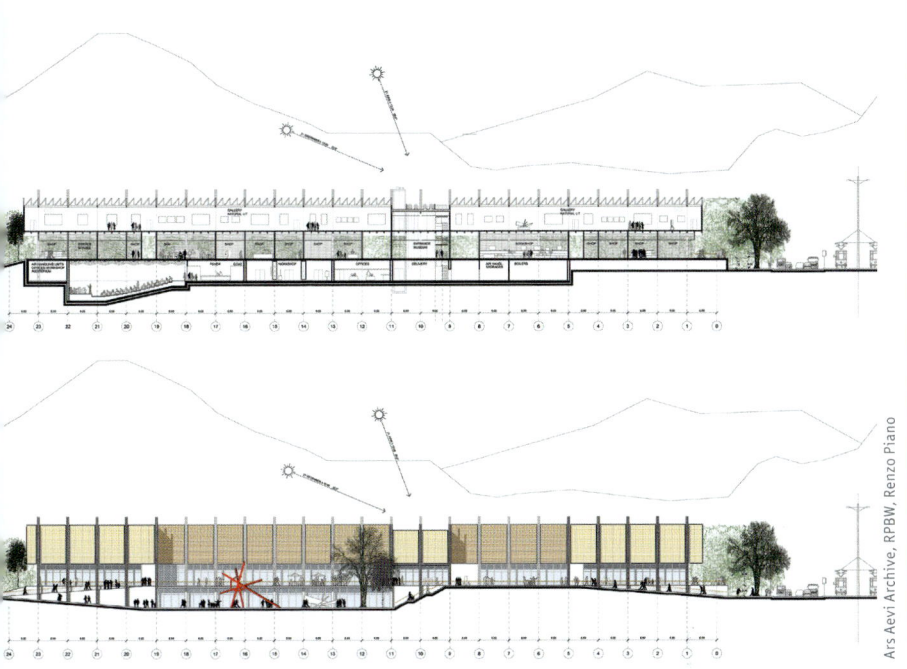

Ars Aevi Archive, RPBW, Renzo Piano

2

Ars Aevi
Museum of Contemporary Art

042 C

Marijin Dvor, Zmaja od Bosne
RPBW, Renzo Piano
since 1999 (in progress)

The project lies on a narrow site between the river and the avenue, aiming to link the residential part of the city on the side of the river with the future university area located on the side of the avenue. The initial plan for the project was to merge the existing Historical Museum building into the new contemporary art museum project. Subsequently, it was decided to leave the old museum untouched and flank the new project to form a more articulate museum pole in which the existing structure could be revitalised. The project runs along a 300-metre-long urban promenade with social and public activities such as a bar, restaurants, a book market, university programmes, and a small hall for temporary exhibitions. This promenade, which begins at a public square among the residential area's buildings, crosses the river by a pedestrian bridge and ends at a large grass field with trees that will become the museum's sculpture garden. At this point, the ramp goes up to the raised platform on which the museum's structure rests. The initial steps for this museum were taken in 2001 with the help of a number of individuals and companies, mostly from Italian cities and regions, who provided materials and services. In 2021, the new Ars Aevi management received support from the City of Sarajevo and the Canton of Sarajevo to proceed with the project, and they were successful in obtaining financing from the Italian government for construction documents. A construction permit is about to be obtained, making building construction more certain than ever. Once complete, this project may revitalise this area while also adding an important layer to Sarajevo's contemporary architecture, as it was designed by the internationally acclaimed architect Renzo Piano.

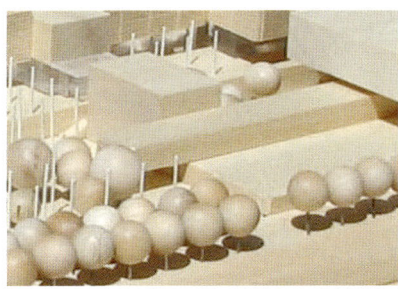

Ars Aevi Archive

Importanne Centre

Marijin Dvor
*Studio Nonstop (Igor Grozdanić
Sanja Galić-Grozdanić)*
2005–2010

The Importanne Centre is a large-scale structure that enhances the main longitudinal axis and elevates the urban atmosphere of Marijin Dvor and contemporary Sarajevo. Studio Nonstop describes it as a 'twenty-first century hybrid' that combines the static nature of a nineteenth-century perimeter block with the dynamic verticality of a twentieth-century office and apartment tower. This fusion is further emphasised through the contextual use of materials, with fibre-cement panels reminiscent of nineteenth-century stucco and glass curtain walls that reference modernist architecture. While each tower possesses its own distinct expression, they come together harmoniously to form a cohesive overall composition. Although the absence of green space is notable, this is compensated for by the inclusion of compact green terraces and vertical gardens. The towers themselves accommodate offices, residences, and a hotel, with each tower functioning and appearing independent, yet integrated within a unified block. They share a base that encompasses three levels of underground parking, topped by three above-ground levels of shopping areas. The transparent nature of the base establishes a clear relationship with the main street, while the eastern tower engages in a formal dialogue with the Historical Museum situated across from it. Despite the western tower remaining unbuilt, the formal integrity of the complex is maintained, effectively shifting the central pedestrian zone of Sarajevo further towards the west than ever before.

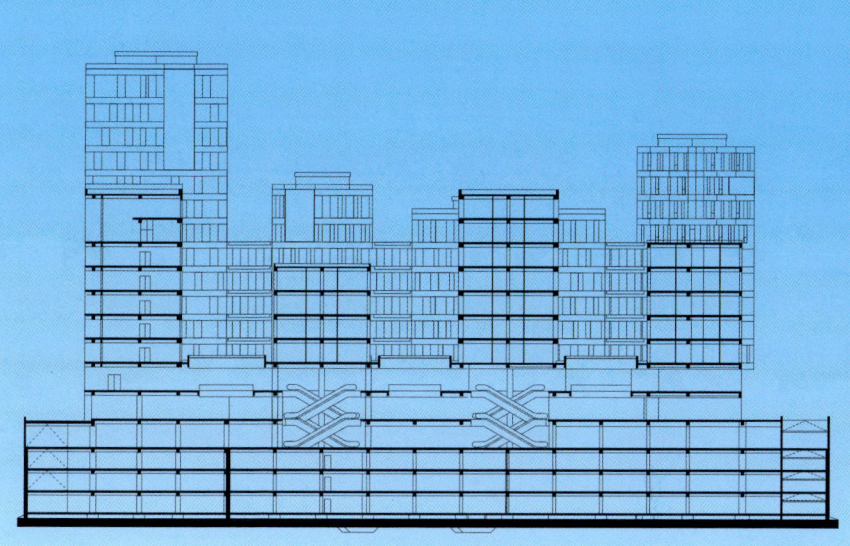

Office Building for UN Agencies

044 **C**

Marijin Dvor, Vilsonovo šetalište
Studio Nonstop (Igor Grozdanić, Sanja Galić-Grozdanić)
2009–2012

Located between the Importanne Centre and Vilsonovo Šetalište recreational street along the Miljacka River, this building serves as one of the five planned business establishments in this area, including diplomatic and consular missions. The design features a symmetrical plan and repetitive façades, which were specifically developed to accommodate the division of all of the above-ground levels into two separate units. This design approach also allows the creation of the office units in various sizes. As a result, the building takes on the form of a simple and rational cube, with white façades and glass windows that showcase a play between solid and void spaces. The meandering lines on the façades create a sense of continuity, connecting one side of the building to another and enhancing the overall unity of the structure. Vertical fluting lines of varying widths adorn the façades, adding a plastic quality and creating a contrast with the reflective windows. The combination of these subtle repetitive façade elements, along with the inverse repetition, contributes to the building's neutral yet distinctive appearance – thoughtful towards the design of the future Ars Aevi Museum of Contemporary Art next to it.

Anida Krečo

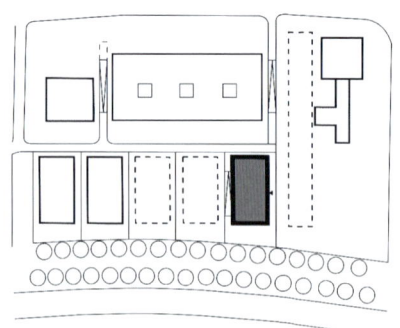

Faculty of Mechanical Engineering
Vilsonovo šetalište 9
Slobodan Jovandić
1985

045 C

The Faculty of Mechanical Engineering was established as an independent unit of the University of Sarajevo in 1984, the same year Slobodan Jovandić presented his proposal for a new building. The new building is composed of four volumetric units. Two horizontal volumes are designated for entrances and public spaces, while the vertical five-storey volume houses classrooms, studios, laboratories, and offices. The largest volume contains amphitheatres and workshops, which are clearly visible on the building's façade. Although the majority of the structure was designed in accordance with architectural standards of that time, characterised by a continuous arrangement of openings and a slightly greater emphasis on volumetric composition rather than the façade design itself, the design of the largest volume stands out the most. The architect played with the composition of the façade by incorporating negative elements that reflect the building's interior, along with numerous galleries and staircases leading to different floors of the building. In this way, a memorable external design was created. Although the façade may appear unfinished, it gives the impression that the amphitheatre extends towards Vilsonova Street, emphasising the entrance sequence and creating a meeting place.

2

Rabbit Wolff

Jeko Ono

Faculty of Natural Sciences and Mathematics

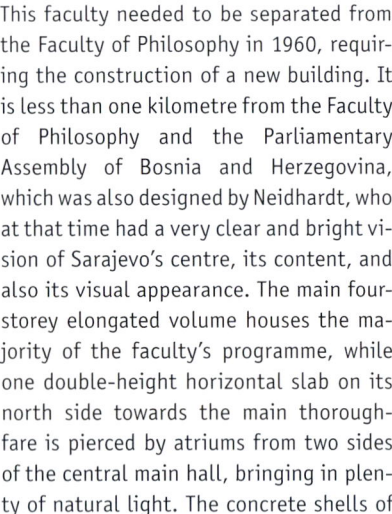

046 **C**

Zmaja od Bosne 33-35
Juraj Neidhardt
1959–1964

This faculty needed to be separated from the Faculty of Philosophy in 1960, requiring the construction of a new building. It is less than one kilometre from the Faculty of Philosophy and the Parliamentary Assembly of Bosnia and Herzegovina, which was also designed by Neidhardt, who at that time had a very clear and bright vision of Sarajevo's centre, its content, and also its visual appearance. The main four-storey elongated volume houses the majority of the faculty's programme, while one double-height horizontal slab on its north side towards the main thoroughfare is pierced by atriums from two sides of the central main hall, bringing in plenty of natural light. The concrete shells of

the amphitheatres for chemistry and physics appear from the horizontal section, culminating in doubly curved roofs. This composition method, 'analogous to traditional learning and based on the principle of contrast of cube and domed elements', was previously elaborated in *Architecture of Bosnia and the Way Towards Modernity*, which dealt with the relationships between Bosnian traditional architecture and modern architecture. Apart from these recognisable amphitheatres, the other distinguishing elements are the slim, stretched-out 'V' pillars that form the building's generously recessed entrance. Following the Šipad Office Building, which had a row of 'V' pillars built a few years before, this principle was supposed to be continuously repeated on other buildings next to the Faculty of Natural Sciences and Mathematics. As a valuable gesture that accounts for Sarajevo's climate, they emerge as a layer of practical and visual urban quality for the city.

Kubus Office Buildings

Zmaja od Bosne 14
Srboslav Stojanović
1980s

047 **C**

These types of buildings were not praised for their architecture in Yugoslav Sarajevo and more emphasis was placed on the companies for which they were designed. This one, named 'Kubusi' ('Cubes'), was created for SIMPO Vranje, a Serbian home furnishings manufacturer and retailer. There was a clear brief to design a building that could house all of the company departments, from administration to retail, as well as a large furniture store, exhibition space, and showroom. The design is based on three distinct but identical volumes that would each house a complementary pair of departments, with the goal of improving the quality of the company's internal processes. As an extension of the pedestrian footpath along the main axis, the architect created a generous public space allowing visitors to circle around completely transparent ground floors of each separate volume. This level hosted retail, exhibition halls, and furniture showrooms, while the top hovering solid volume was used for offices and storage. Although the proportional and material relationship between these two levels seems comparable to that of the Historical Museum, it is distinguished by its chamfering in details as well as at four corners where it captures more natural light. Following the 1990s war, a fourth identical building was constructed as a separate one with minor differences in detail from the first three. Despite the fact that today they have been labelled and divided by various company offices and shops, their scale, repetition, and public accessibility make them stand out among other buildings along the main axis.

2

Pasha Oko

Energoinvest Office Tower

048 C

Hamdije Čemerlića 2
Alija Serdarević
1976–1979

The massive Energoinvest building, located on the northeast corner of a significant industrial location from the Yugoslav era, serves as a striking reminder of the important engineering and industrial company that once thrived within its walls. With a rich history of doing business all over the world, Energoinvest was renowned as the largest exporter in the former Yugoslavia, boasting an impressive workforce of 42,000 employees. Comprising of a vertical business tower and a five-story building along the street, the architecture of the Energoinvest building seamlessly blends functionality with aesthetics. The park setting surrounding the lower building creates a harmonious transition to the main entrance, offering a pleasant environment for visitors and employees alike. The tower itself is a testament to architectural ingenuity, as it is split into two asymmetrical mirror halves by vertical communications. Its façade, adorned with a distinctive brown finishing colour, echoes the design choices of other buildings constructed during the same period. However, the fully developed large-scale nature of the Energoinvest building, coupled with its chamfered corners, grants it a unique and captivating allure. While the building's roundness softens its mass, it still retains a monumental presence within its surroundings, showcasing a blend of strength and elegance. Over the years, Energoinvest has undergone significant downsizing, resulting in the consolidation of its main office premises in the lower five-storey building. This transition, however, has not diminished the building's significance. In a recent development, the government of the Federation of Bosnia and Herzegovina claimed ownership of the tower, further underscoring its spatial adaptability and symbolic importance in the city's landscape.

Studio SWITCH

S2 Residential-Office Building

049 **C**

Zmaja od Bosne 47
Kemal Hasibović
2012–2015

The immediate surroundings had a significant impact on the character of the S2 complex. The main factors that affected the building's disposition, materialisation, and form included its proximity to administrative facilities, frequent traffic, business city hotels, and recently opened shopping and business centres. The building has a square base and three distinct volumes. Each volume has its own height and shape, and when combined, they create a dynamic composition that faces Zmaja od Bosne Street, Sarajevo's main thoroughfare. The slightly fragmented structural façade reflects its surroundings, which, along with the shifting monochromatic tones of the glass fields, contributes to the façade's own dynamics. The interior of the building reflects its character as well; it can be configured for any programme thanks to a vertical concrete communications core in the middle. The building currently houses a variety of programmes, including the offices of state institutions, commercial entities, and residential apartments, in addition to an underground garage with 340 parking spaces.

2

Studio SWITCH

Environmental Fund of the Federation of BiH (Vodoprivreda) ↓

050 C

Hamdije Ćemerlića 39a
Vladimir Zarahović, Dragan Bijedić, Zijo Krvavac
2000

Psh Oko

This 12-storey glass building was constructed as part of the capital's post-war infrastructure rebuilding efforts in the 1990s. Situated along the Vilsonovo Šetalište recreational area on the Miljacka River, it reflects the surroundings and stands out in contrast to the otherwise uniform background of the Grbavica residential neighbourhood. Its modest volumetric composition resembles its company logo.

Pasha Oko

Šibica Residential Building →

051 C

Ložionička
Unknown architect
1960s

One of the buildings along the main axis is the Šibica Residential Building or the 'Matchbox' tower, as it is known among the citizens who mock the size and shape of the building. Slender on one side and wide on the other, the residential tower of 20 floors protrudes in an otherwise moderately scaled residential neighbourhood. The significance and symbolism of the building rose even more during the wartime years of the 1990s when parts of it burned due to constant shelling. In the aftermath of the war, it was mostly neglected. Some emergency repairs were completed, but the major works on changing its appearance were done by the inhabitants

Health Insurance Institute of Sarajevo Canton (Socijalno)

052 C

Ložionička 2
Živorad Janković, Esad Daidžić
1960

In the early 1960s, this part of Sarajevo had no city plan, therefore the building's shape was determined by its programme and appearance. It consists of three interconnected units: the 11-storey unit, the one-story unit, both housing different types of offices, and the 'Arena' cinema, which functioned as an individual unit. At the time of construction, public savings were requested, which affected the building's net area and final decor. However, as soon as the skeleton was built, the building's importance was obvious so additional funds were set aside for façade upgrades.

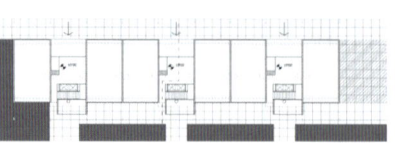

Ana Sužnjević

themselves. Partial façade reconstructions, enclosed balconies, colourful windows, and various other interventions, along with the war scars created a new symbolism depicting the time we live in.

Headquarters of B&H Public Electricity Utility Company (Elektroprivreda)

053 C

Vilsonovo šetalište 15
Ivan Štraus
1978

This building played an important role in the development of Sarajevo, not only because of its memorable and distinctive architecture, but also because of its position in the urban matrix of the city. As at the time it was designed, this area was quite unurbanised, and there were no inherited or historic urban structures to use as a reference. The architect was quite free to introduce the contemporary formability and materialisation characteristic of the late 1970s architecture in the city. The building consists of three distinct volumes that represent not only the functional division between departments of the company, but also a specific symbolism connected to the process of making electricity. The three volumes are characterised by three distinctive colours: yellow, blue, and green, which were added after its post-war renovation. Before the war, all three volumes featured bronze-gold reflective glass panels. The renovation process resulted in the architect coming up with new colours

and their symbolism. The yellow volume is a five-storey cubical office building that represents the administrative building of a hydroelectric power plant; the blue two-storey horizontal volume hosts public relations and inquiries and represents a river flowing through the imaginary power plant; and green volume, an eight-storey administrative building, represents the dam that controls the flow of water through an imaginary power plant, finishing with a fountain at a small plaza. Using a reduced spectrum of materials – only raw concrete and reflective glass on aluminium girders – the architect wanted to put focus on the formability of this imposing structure, topping everything off with a concrete cap – a characteristic element of his architectural style that can be seen on UNITIC Towers and the Holiday Inn Hotel, where he positioned the service and maintenance floor. The upside-down cascading form became iconic and recognisable in the city's silhouette.

2

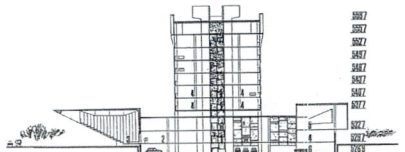

Ivan Štraus Archive

Pasha Oko

Block 29 Residential Building 054 B

Malta nn
Nikola Maslej, Sulejman Midžić
1983

As the common typology of high-density housing architecture in Sarajevo at the time, a skyscraper known as the Block 29 Residential Building introduced a different concept at one of the important intersections in the Dolac Malta neighbourhood. It is designed as a semi-open block that mirrors the street corner and is pushed back to create physical distance from the busy street. It is commonly known as Kifla ('crescent roll') among locals because the aerial view of its shape is reminiscent of a Balkan crescent roll. Block 29 or Kifla has eight residential storeys with working-class apartments as well as an extended public ground floor that spans two storeys. Despite repetitive floors and standard apartments, there is a clear intention to lessen repetition and create more variability. The bright main volume is decomposed with recessed parts in colour, while window elements break their logic, creating more identifiable portions of its façades. Later, a two-storey concave commercial building was added in front of this convex building, forming a unique urban composition in Sarajevo.

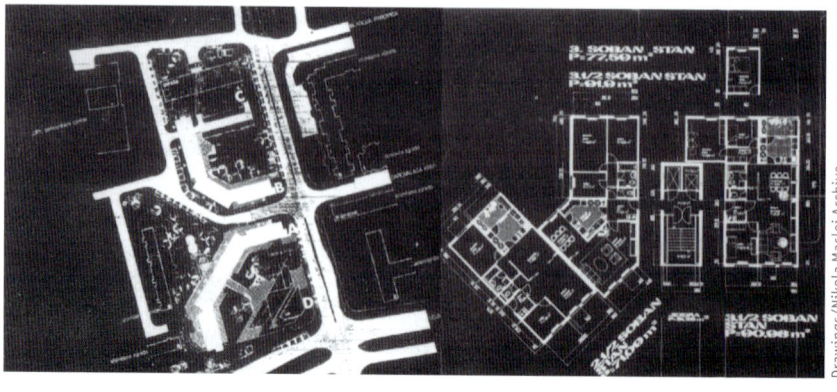

Drawings/Nikola Maslej Archive

Izautin Pašić

Post Office Dolac Malta

055 C

Zmaja od Bosne 14
Ahmet Kapidžić
1976

At the time of construction, Sarajevo was rapidly expanding westward, and public service companies needed to expand and build new facilities. Along with the headquarters of the B&H Public Electricity Utility Company and others, this new Post Office was built in the Dolac Malta neighbourhood. While the two buildings follow the logic of the upside-down cascading building, the Post Office is not only smaller in scale and placed parallel to the street, but its section also changes not on the scale of the detail. All aboveground storeys expand across the perimeter of the previous floor, while the repetitive concrete vertical elements between windows appear to hold the expansion above, creating an illusion that the building is floating. It is reminiscent of the 1969 Boston City Hall in terms of typology and details, as both buildings have courtyards and purely brutalistic exposed concrete elements as their main formal features. Although the inner courtyard of the Post Office is not open to the public, it does have an unusual feature for Sarajevo: a large public space surrounding it.

Bosmal City Centre

056 B

Milana Preloga 12
Sead Gološ (Grupa Arh)
2001–2009

This complex of 118-metre-tall business and residential towers with a total area of 35,000 m² was considered the largest foreign direct investment in Sarajevo at the time the project began. Two L-shaped towers stand atop a plinth that houses a commercial zone on six floors between the garage's final level and the installation storey below the towers' apartments. One tower is topped by a circular floating heliodrome, while another has a peculiar form that wraps double-height floors with a 360-degree view of Sarajevo and its surroundings. The towers were constructed as reinforced concrete frame structures on a foundation slab with reinforced concrete piles. The overlapping

Vedad Krkbešević

portions of coloured glazed, aluminium, and plaster façades affect the perception of the towers' scale. Although the massive towers appear cramped at the beginning of the steep hill where a completely different typology and scale of buildings begin, the Bosmal Towers remain one of the region's tallest buildings.

2

Pasha Oko

Health Centre Novi Grad (Kumrovec)

057 B

Bulevar Meše Selimovića 2
Zdravko Likić, Nikola Bašić
1975

The Health Centre's two horizontal volumes stretch parallel to Sarajevo's main thoroughfare, floating above the open car park by original design, with an in-between entry platform accessible via a monumental staircase. When it was built, this strategy of naturally ventilating the health service building by providing outdoor access to specific departments, as well as a network of wide corridors and bold visual communications, was recognised as a remarkable quality, as described in *15 years of Bosnian-Herzegovinian Architecture* in 1987. After being used for 40 years and suffering damage by the war and the weather, a great deal of knowledge about climate, maintenance, and building physics was gained. When the building was completely renovated in 2016, the entry platform was completely enclosed, and the majority of the ground level car park was converted into new entrances and an indoor area. Unlike most recent city renovations, this one made an effort to preserve the original exterior materiality, combining red aluminium plates in place of the brick façade and white ones to highlight the former horizontal concrete strokes. Despite the conceptual shift, the impression of the sleek two-storey horizontal volumes detached from the ground remained, emphasising Sarajevo's main axis.

Kumrovec II
Residential-Office Building

 058 B

Džemala Bijedića 25
Lejla Hasibović, Kemal Hasibović
2015–2016

The building's location is part of the 'Čengić Vila II' urban neighbourhood. An internal road surrounds it to the north, with the Bulevar Meše Selimović main axis to the south, and residential and commercial structures to the east and west. Six staircases connect the garage in the basement and the entry area on the ground floor to the first three floors, which are divided into four lamellas. Aside from the entrances to the upper residential floors, all of the commercial spaces are on the ground floor and its gallery. With its length of 125 metres, this building along with the Radio and Television Building contributes to the urban atmosphere of Sarajevo's main street. The two higher parts of the building appear to relate to nearby residential skyscrapers in a repetitive rhythm, which demonstrates sensitivity to the existing residential environment. While the solid white and glazed grey stripes appear to be repeated from a distance, the unambitious sensitivity is evident in the detail of various widths, which seem to repeat the volumetric pattern. This project shows that architectural design can add value in small, subtle ways, even when it has to meet a maximum square footage requirement.

2

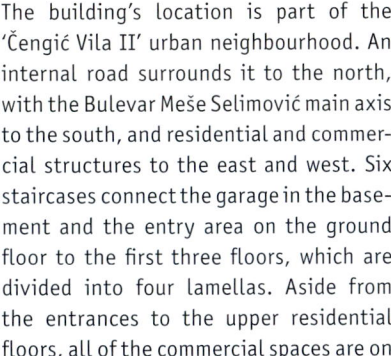

Studio SWITCH

Radio and Television Building

Meše Selimovića 12
Milan Kušan,
Branko Bulić
1975-1983

The first initiatives to design the Sarajevo Radio and Television Building began in 1965 at a time when the country lacked significant project experience in this type of building, so the final conceptual design was completed only in 1968. The basic concept was based on enabling phased construction due to the large-scale contents, i.e., over 100,000 m² on a plot of approximately 7 ha. The programme was divided into three major architectural units – the production-reproduction facility, the business facility, and the operating facility – and each of these units, with the exception of the business facility, is designed to allow for phased construction. Measuring approximately 22,000 m², the first stage was completed in 1974 – a pioneering undertaking as the country's first television facility, completely newly built and designed by local experts. The authors received significant social recognition when they were nominated by Bosnia and Herzegovina for the Borba Award, a prestigious annual award presented by *Borba* magazine in collaboration with the Association of Architects of Yugoslavia for the best urban-architectural realisation in Yugoslavia. Following the success of Sarajevo's bid

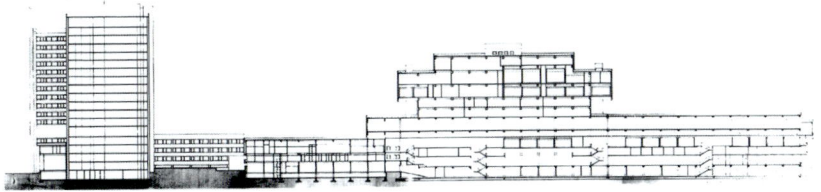

to host the 1984 Winter Olympics, preparations for the design and construction of the International RTV Centre, one of the key buildings, began. This new phase did not significantly change the basic design concept from 1968, with only minor changes in disposition within the dimensions already determined by the first stage, proving the viability of the approach and the system's overall flexibility. The building is distinguished by long horizontal layers of concrete and windows that stretch out over 300 m along the main thoroughfare, culminating in a rectangular tower that dominates the surrounding street level. It became known as the 'Grey House' (Sivi Dom) because of its imposing concrete brutalist structure. The bold and brave architecture of the Radio and Television Building, as well as its dramatic and important role in history during the Winter Olympics and during the war of the 1990s, made it a truly unique landmark of Sarajevo.

2

Michael Walczak

Alipašino Polje Settlement

060 B

Ive Andrića, Geteova,
Semira Fraste

*Milan Medić, Jug Milić,
Zdravko Likić, Sanja Galić,
Halid Muhasilović, Srbislav
Stojanović, Šaćir Omerović, Kemal Tanović,
Ognjeslav Malkin, Enes Sabljaković*
1978–1980

The Alipašino Polje settlement comprises two distinct clusters of residential blocks, each thoughtfully adapting to the surrounding terrain and urban context. It is characterised by a series of buildings, while vehicular traffic primarily occupies the peripheral roads. Meanwhile, the spaces between the buildings has been designed as pedestrian zones, adorned with lines of green areas and squares. In accordance with contemporary urban planning principles, the design of the settlement embraced the concept of a moving sequence, both horizontally and vertically, fostering volumetric dynamism within the structures. The aim of the settlement's design was twofold: to maximise space utilisation and construction efficiency, while simultaneously providing a substantial number of residential units. Significantly, the construction of the Alipašino Polje settlement brought

2

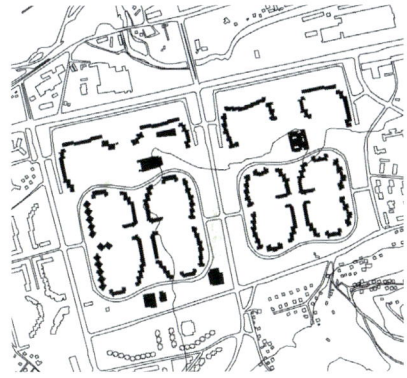

together numerous professional and social forces, all united in their desire to
showcase the capabilities of the socialist state in terms of urban planning, architectural excellence, and the technical
feasibility of such a large-scale settlement project. The settlement is composed
of three distinct neighbourhoods: Phase
A, B, and C, each encompassing six local
communities. Construction took place between 1978 and 1980, a period marked by
rapid urbanisation and an urgent need
for a substantial number of apartments.
With a grand total of 8,250 apartments, it
stands as the largest singular complex in
Sarajevo. Construction was undertaken by
esteemed contractors such as GP Vranica,
GP Bosna, and ŽGP Sarajevo. The built
structures occupy 23.5 per cent of the
gross realised area, construction sites account for 23.72 per cent, and the remaining 53.03 per cent is dedicated to open
spaces. At the heart of the settlement
lie communal areas, squares, green spaces, and walkways. During the war, these
green areas served as fertile fields for cul-
tivating vegetables. Over time, despite
previously carrying a reputation for being crowded and less desirable compared
to other residential zones, the Alipašino
Polje settlement has gained increasing
appeal as an attractive place to reside.

Student Housing in Nedžarići   061 B

Aleja Bosne Srebrene nn
Enver Jahić
1971

There is a student dormitory with a capacity of 5,000 beds in the Nedžarići neighbourhood in the western part of the city. The distinctive Y-shaped design of the dormitory is achieved through three volumes of residential space, with an additional ground floor volume with public and service areas. Vertical communication is positioned at the junction of the three prism-like volumes, facilitating communication and orientation for the students. Longitudinal corridors between the two tracts of rooms serve as horizontal communication pathways. One tract exclusively consists of double rooms, while the other tract is dedicated to triple rooms with anterooms. The anteroom areas feature closets and sinks, while showers and toilets are shared. The residential pavilion comprises eight floors, each with four housing groups on every level. Social spaces, including the restaurant and kitchen, are located on the mezzanine level of the dormitory. The construction of the facility involved the use of monolithic reinforced concrete slabs, enabling a swift realisation.

Radon Plaza Hotel (Oslobođenje Headquarters)   062 B

Džemala Bijedića 185
Mladen Gvozden, Kenan Šahović
(initial design) 1982
Faruk Kapidžić, Ahmet Kapidžić
(reconstruction, redesign) 2005

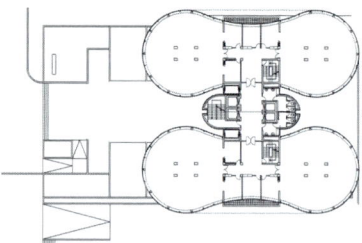

The short life of the *Oslobođenje* newspaper HQ ended at the beginning of the 1990s. The cubic forms were replaced by curved ones in 2005 when it was reconstructed; the central core and structures were kept, and the rest of the building was renovated. Form and material changed, as did the purpose, changing to hospitality. It is now one of the best hotels in the city with 117 rooms, one presidential suite, a wellness area, a pool, and a rotating restaurant at the top.

ADS Stduio

Retirement Home (Dom Penzionera) ↓

Džemala Bijedića nn, Ilidža
Mladen Gvozden
1987–1992

There is a derelict and dilapidated complex of colourful buildings in the Nedžarići neighbourhood in the west of Sarajevo. However, while they appear marginalised and forlorn now, these ruins were once a bold representative of post-modernism in Sarajevo. The competition for the conceptual design was won by the Sarajevo architect Mladen Gvozden from Arhitekt and the project was completed in 1992 after five years of construction. It consisted of 16,000 square metres of floor space and contained 150 beds. A seven-level tower next to the apartments included not only residential services for the elderly, but also an intensive care unit and a dedicated morgue in the tower's basement. Upon completion, it was among the most ambitious and innovative retirement communities in the country. When construction on the complex was completed in 1992, several dozen pensioners were preparing to move into the facility, though this never happened as the war started. Today, it is clear that the complex will soon be demolished and replaced with something new.

In addition to serving as a student dormitory, the building also accommodates other public amenities, emphasising its multifunctional character.

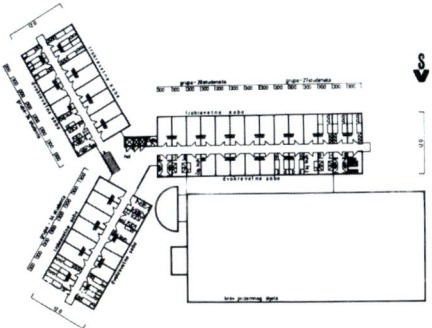

Dobrinja Settlement (Olympic Village)

064 B

Bulevar branilaca Dobrinje nn
Milan Medić
1982–1990

The Olympics were the high point of Yugoslav history, and especially so in the aftermath of President Tito's death in 1980. The 1984 Winter Olympic Games brought the region under the spotlight. In order to host thousands of athletes, coaches, media personnel, and tourists, Sarajevo underwent thorough reconstruction and (re)development. Dobrinja, located right across from Sarajevo Airport, was chosen as a future Olympic neighbourhood. Often taken for granted in the creation of Olympic villages, the temporality aspect was questioned early in the process. All that was to be built for the purpose of housing during the games was cleverly adapted to be transformed into permanent residences for the increasing population of Sarajevo thereafter. Built in less than two years, Dobrinja Olympic Village is defined as two residential neighbourhoods with 2,100 housing units distributed across high-rise towers

and smaller-scale apartment blocks. The village planned for a school, as well as laying base principles for the future town square and the main promenade. Compared to Sarajevo's previous urban housing developments in the 1970s, including Grbavica, Dobrinja's entire environment is far larger and more orderly in design. Its layout is distinguished by a carefully planned grid system of streets and buildings, which includes plenty of green space in the middle of each block. Neighbourhoods of Dobrinja I and II were so successful that III, IV, and V followed consecutively in the late 1980s and early 1990s, with 40,000 people. It is now home to four primary and two secondary schools and is a vibrant settlement with many young people choosing to live here.

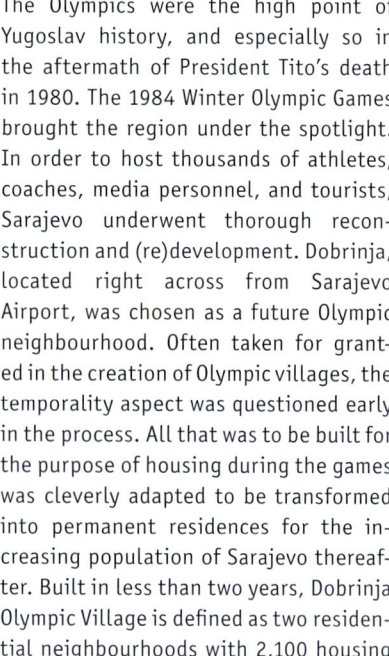

Sarajevo International Airport

065 B

Kurta Schorka 36
Hasan Ćemalović, Nikola Nešković (initial design) 1984
Sead Gološ, (Grupa Arh; extension) 2023

Sarajevo Airport grew and expanded organically as the city grew, with several distinguished periods in its lifetime coinciding with historical events. The first flights arrived in 1930 on an unpaved stretch of stamped earth with a trivial terminal building – Butmir Airport. An idea for a new contemporary airport was put forward after the Second World War with the increase in numbers of tourists arriving to the region. The first terminal, a glass pavilion, was constructed in 1969 on the site of the old airport. It served four gates and was demolished in 2017 to make space for the latest expansion. The terminal in use today was initially built to cover the needs of hosting the 1984 Winter Olympics. The new terminal services up to one million passengers per year. The introverted cubical form is pierced lengthwise by a prominent glass prism, functioning as a skylight, giving lightness to and visually expanding the interior space. The cubicle is clad in polished grey stone with an offset glass cutout on the front featuring entrance/exit doors and accentuated with bright blue frames. The main hall is a double-height space with a gallery and access bridges. During the 1990s, the airport acted as a border of the siege zone, with humanitarian flights replacing civilian ones. Fast forward 30 years, the airport has outgrown its capacity. Sead Gološ (Grupa Arh) designed a new expansion and added a 155-metre-long sculptural canopy to visually unite the existing building with the new addition, as well as to expand the airport waiting area to the outside. The canopy has a broken triangular form covered in mirror-like polished aluminium to reflect the traffic beneath. The latest expansion is directly connected to the central area of the existing building and has a three-storey atrium with similar materialisation to the existing building and seamless material crossovers.

2

Sloven Avdibović

Informal Sarajevo
Catch the Diversity

Informal Sarajevo captures the architecture of the Formal Sarajevo zone and the main city thoroughfare. This part of the city is built from the axis and up towards Sarajevo's hillsides. Here, the city responds to the topography in its peculiar ways, with its controlled and organically expanding typologies, urban and semi-urban quarters, ladder streets, terraced housing complexes, and regionally and topographically influenced modernist architectural works, all contributing to a vibrant Sarajevo visual appearance.

Informal Sarajevo explores this identity through its in-betweens, its tucked and hidden parts, specific and non-standard approaches, even adding in kiosks with their ever-changing locations around the city. This chapter showcases a heterogenous Sarajevo in terms of architectural approaches and geographical locations, with dozens of projects exploring the distinct juxtaposing of the built environment and expressive topography.

It starts in the Old Town with a Kovači plateau and a recent administrative building paraphrasing tradition and preserving genius loci through modernist expression. It moves on to the Kopčić

Family house, a well-proportioned early modernist building seamlessly integrating into the surroundings of the historical Sarajevo residential area, and then towards the sensitive approach in Ghazi Husrev-Bey's Hamam Shops, and the Vakuf Hovaža Kemaludin building, representing one of the most significant avant-garde achievements of modernity in the period between the two world wars. This chapter also covers megaprojects like the Ciglane Residential Complex built in 1989 in several continuous volumes, or as authors refer to it 'urbarchitecture', and Olympic hall ZETRA, to this day the largest sports complex in Bosnia and Herzegovina. The Informal chapter concludes with recently built projects at the southern slopes of Mt. Trebević where the border between the city and the mountains blurs. For most of the sites, walking combined with public transport is recommended, as driving and finding parking in dense hillside areas is an art of its own. If walking, this chapter should be explored in parallel with the Formal Sarajevo chapter, as the locations and distances between the various sites and buildings overlap. Use the map as your main guide for the walk.

3

Destination Sarajevo

Gazi Husrev-beg's Bezistan

View from Bjelave towards the city centre, with the mountains of Bjelašnica and Igman in the background

3

Nina Ugljen-Ademović

Memorial Fund Amphitheatre Kovači

066 D

Ploče nn
Namik Mufitć, Aida Daidžić
1998–2017

The Fond Memorijala amphitheatre is part of the second phase of the Shehid Memorial Centre Kovači. Besides being one of the biggest multimedia conference halls in Sarajevo with 350 seats, the amphitheatre hosts a Memorial Wall with the names of all detected shehids and victims of the 1990s war as part of the entrance sequence. The project was commissioned through an open public competition in 1998. A bird's eye perspective reveals its large-scale oriental motifs. Besides the amphitheatre and conference hall, the complex hosts a cemetery, a museum, parts of the historical defence walls, and the administration building for the Fond Memorijala offices.

Vedad Krkbešević

Administrative Building Rijaset of the Islamic Community in Bosnia and Herzegovina

067 D

Kovači 36
Zlatko Ugljen
2008–2022

The Rijaset administrative building is on the Kovači plateau, which has a special position and topological attributes, but is also symbolic and has historical significance. On the surrounding slopes of the Vratnik settlement towards the Kovači plateau, significant positions are occupied by medieval and Ottoman buildings of Bijela tabija and Žuta tabija, as well as Jajce barracks, an Austro-Hungarian military facility that towers over the old part of the city. The author clearly states the relationship to the buildings mentioned in the explanation of the concept, describing the building of Rijaset 'as the

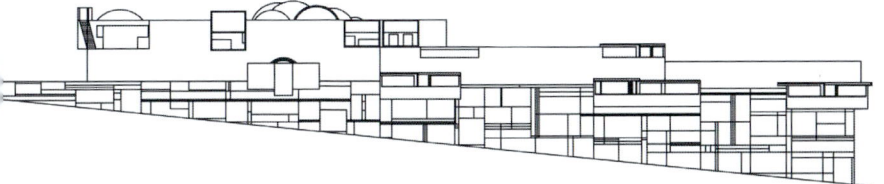

ending of Kovači, the one that announces the trinity in form and historical flow'. The building attempts to paraphrase tradition by adjusting to significant historical objects and preserving the genius loci through the expression of contemporary architecture. The dominant ground volume along Kovači Street is lined with stone blocks with relief element pauses as a reference to the old town walls of Vratnik Gate, creating a striking transition from the public street to the building's inner plateau. This relationship is softened by the repeated white volumes with pergolas as a reference to *doksat* (a projecting part of a building) and also to typical gardens of the Vratnik and Kovači landscape. Aside from the ground volume, which houses an auditorium, garage, and service facilities, the rest of the building is composed of two ground-floor and one single-storey volume. The ground floor is designed for administration, with meeting and conference rooms, and the highest level is for the offices of the head of the Islamic Community of Bosnia and Herzegovina, reception rooms, and roof gardens providing panoramic views of the Old Town to the east and south, as well as the newer Sarajevo to the west.

3

Novidnska agencija MINA

Timur Babić

Gazi-Husrev Bey Library
Gazi Husrev-begova 46
Kenan Šahović
2014

068 D

The oldest library in Bosnia officially, founded around 1537, is now housed in a new and contemporarily furnished building specifically designed for this purpose. The original library fund was gathered in the sixteenth century for educational purposes in the newly founded Madrassah, as desired by the owner of the legacy – Gazi Husrev Bey. The library can be accessed through a few points. The first entrance is in Gazi Husrev-beg Street through a monumental wooden door framed with geometric decorations. It is placed at

the top of a staircase, lifting it from street level. The entire façade at this point is covered in white stone and given very subtle, mostly geometric decorations, along with some oriental insignia. The left side also has a window with stained glass decorated in the same manner, and a few small shops that are ubiquitous to Čaršija. The interior of the library contains a large auditorium under the dome, spanning the height of two floors, several reading rooms, as well as specialised spaces for the preservation of books and manuscripts. The vestibule and courtyard of the library are open to visitors during the day, and the complex also houses two small museums, while the entire library fund is digitalised and available online.

Jeko Ono

3

Kopčić Family House
 069 D

Safet Bega Bašagića 48
Reuf Kadić
1939

The Kopčić Family House represents a well-proportioned early modern house that seamlessly integrates into the surroundings of the old Sarajevo residential area. With its adjacent walled courtyard and cantilevered upper floor, traditional Bosnian house features have been skilfully adjusted for contemporary use. It also presents the successful use of locally available materials at the time it was built. An upper floor corner loggia is partially glazed and has a distinct railing on the open side. Built even before Dušan Grabrijan and Juraj Neidhardt published the book *Architecture of Bosnia and the Way Towards Modernity*, it is one of the finest examples of Moderna residences designed by Reuf Kadić.

Gazi Husrev-Bey's Hamam Shops ←
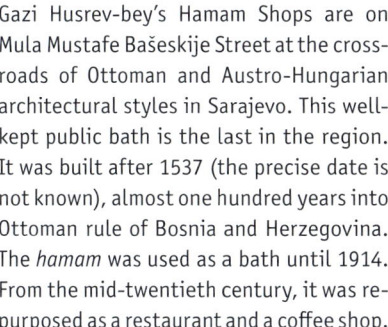 070 D

Mula Mustafe Bašeskije 21
Ahmed Džuvić
2001

Gazi Husrev-bey's Hamam Shops are on Mula Mustafe Bašeskije Street at the crossroads of Ottoman and Austro-Hungarian architectural styles in Sarajevo. This well-kept public bath is the last in the region. It was built after 1537 (the precise date is not known), almost one hundred years into Ottoman rule of Bosnia and Herzegovina. The *hamam* was used as a bath until 1914. From the mid-twentieth century, it was repurposed as a restaurant and a coffee shop.

Architect Ahmed Džuvić was commissioned to design an extension with shops leaning on it towards the main street. It is fully designed in wood, excluding the metal joints, anchors, and roofing tiles. Unlike traditional shops at Baščaršija, these are fully glazed toward the street, featuring the sensitive zenithal light detail next to the *hamam's* wall. The design of the metal anchors is particularly interesting as it showcases the architect's well thought through design process, while the timber construction represents a contemporary take on local traditional timber architecture. This contemporary add-on to a historic building and a national monument is considered one of the most valued after the 1990s.

Turkish Cultural Centre

071 D

Mula Mustafe Bašeskije 31/a
Studio ZEC
2003

The Turkish Cultural Centre is on Mula Mustafe Bašeskije's narrow main street, right next to the tram line. The street is lined with Austro-Hungarian buildings on the left and old buildings of indeterminate character on the right; it is a diverse streetscape typical of Sarajevo within the protected zone defined by the master plan for the Čaršija. The 1,000-square-metre building had to fit on a site only 8 metres wide and 32 metres deep, leaving only one façade to the main street. The author makes references to Eastern philosophy, so entering the building is important for understanding its essence. A glazed inner courtyard connects the small building to the front, whose number of storeys was determined by planning regulations. A *sokak* ('a narrow side street') to the right leads to the *avlija* ('the inner spacious courtyard') and then into the house. The first floor is made up of galleries, culminating in a barrel-vaulted café-tea house with views of the city's roofs in the distance. The *doksat* ('a projecting part of a building'), the most striking element of Ottoman Turkish architecture that encloses the Turkish room on the first floor, dominates and constitutes the street front.

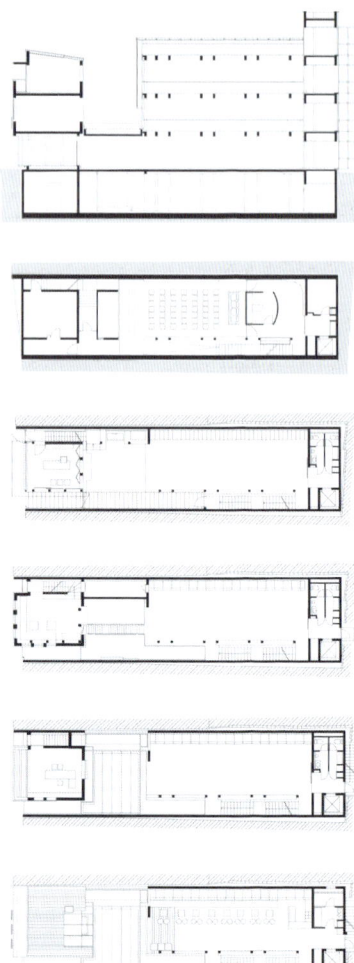

Sandro Lendler

Sandro Lendler

Kibe Mahala Restaurant
Vrbanjuša 106
Studio ZEC
2012

072 B

3

Kibe Restaurant was created as an extension of a family house and this defined the atmosphere it is famous for – traditional cuisine in a cozy, home-like atmosphere with a panoramic view of Sarajevo. Formerly a residential house and later a restaurant, the project gained new spatial potential by merging two buildings into one. The designed solution for Kibe Mahala extends the existing space by expanding the southern part of the ground floor. Looking at the cross section, below the expansion of the restaurant volume lies the reception and auxiliary rooms of the inn, connected by the staircase volume with rooms, a garage, and a souvenir shop. Kibe Restaurant therefore became Kibe Mahala, growing into three connected wholes: house-restaurant, garden-yard, inn-souvenir shop. The elements of a traditional house are present in the stone ground floor, the *doksat*, the white façade of the first floor with a paraphrase of *mušebak*, and the powerful eaves, all expressed in a modern architectural vocabulary and responses to contemporary needs. Kibe Mahala presents an interesting proposal to the *mahala* itself and is an example of how to subsequently intervene into the unplanned constructed tissue.

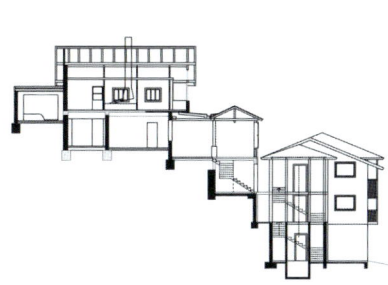

Anida Krečo

Timur Babić

Hotel Europe

Vladislava Skarića 9
Sead Gološ (Grupa Arh)
2007

073 D

The Hotel Europe (Evropa) was built in 1882 during the period of Austro-Hungarian rule in Bosnia-Herzegovina as one of the biggest and the first modern hotel in the country. It is in the heart of Sarajevo's Old Town and was designed by Czech-born architect Karel Pařík. Hotel Europe's structure was protected and sanitised from further decay by the late 1990s and it reopened on its 126th birthday in 2007. The lead architect during the refurbishment was Sead Gološ and his Grupa Arh firm. In the part of the building where the hotel facilities are organised,

two environments were designed in two parts of the hotel, namely: the Austro-Hungarian part with an ambience reminiscent of the period in which the hotel was built, with classically decorated interiors, high ceilings, upholstered walls, wall coverings with wooden panels; and the new part of the hotel with contemporary interior elements of clean and simple lines and forms.

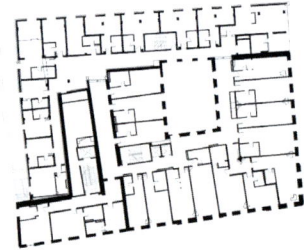

Hotel Opal

Despićeva 4
*AHAKNAP + SAAHA
(Kenan Brčkalija,
Adnan Harambašić)*
2014

074 D

A small boutique hotel by the Bosnian-Norwegian architectural practice AHAKNAP + SAAHA sits in the historic heart of the city just a few minutes' walk from the Latin Bridge or Ferhadija Street. The project is a transformation of a previously underused slim administrative building, which with its volume, façade, and roof shape stood out in its surroundings. The full height of the building was preserved; however, a heavy, overaccentuated attic volume was removed,

resulting in a seemingly lower building. The remnant of the narrow, six-storey volume was kept and further changes set within the existing structural raster. The openings were vertically extended to span between the slabs, resulting in big glass portals. On the outside, a reticent, vertically striated façade was added to create a respectful backdrop for the historic city, as well as a new expression for the building. The vertical wooden ribs provide intimacy behind the windows, while letting enough daylight in. The hotel has 12 rooms fitted with oak tree interiors and a restaurant – part of an appropriated ground floor of a neighbouring building. The repeating floorplan is crowned with a recognisable AHAKNAP + SAAHA element – a rooftop terrace.

Vakuf Čokadži Hadži Sulejman
Ćemaluša
Reuf Kadić
1938–1939

075 D

The building is located at the beginning of the Bistrik settlement and was built as a free-standing structure on sloping terrain. It is modularly uniform and has a very harmonious shape. Polygonal floor plans have total dimensions of 23.6 m × 24 m. The building is made up of the ground floor plus three floors, while the basement also appears on the southern part of the building. The two floors above the ground floor have large, glazed corner loggias and, in combination with the recessed and largely glazed ground floor, create the impression of a light, floating cube, which is one of the characteristics of modern buildings. Business premises are planned on the north side of the ground floor, while the rest of the building has a residential function. Glazed loggias, used for the first time in this building, became a frequently used element in later projects. The integration of all elements characterises this very successful project. The foundations of Čokadži Sulejman were included in the list of national monuments of Bosnia and Herzegovina in November 2011.

Emir Kadić Archive

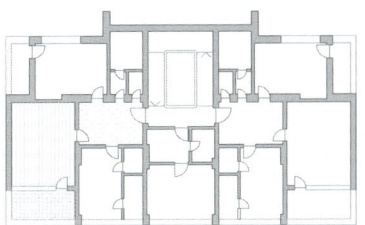

Elša Turkušić

3

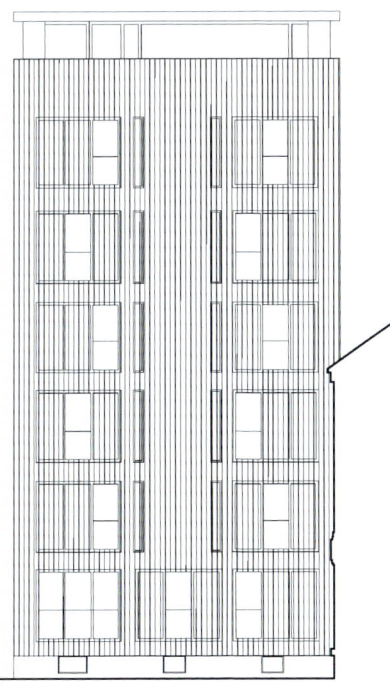

Anida Krečo

Jeko Ono

Municipality Old Town

Zelenih beretki 4
Zoran Brož, 1980
Unknown, 2020

076 D

The municipal building Stari Grad (Old Town) of Sarajevo has been the subject of extensive debate over the years. Following its construction in 1980, the building's youthful architect, Zoran Brož, received two prestigious awards presented in the former Yugoslavia. It is discreetly nestled amid Zelenih Beretki Street, the Armed Forces of Bosnia and Herzegovina Hall, the National Art Gallery of Bosnia and Herzegovina, and the tranquil Miljacka River. Comprising three distinct volumes, the edifice harmoniously integrates into the existing urban fabric, forming an urban insertion. Notably, its distinctive design has resulted in the creation of a network of interconnected back alleys and mezzanine skywalks. During the 1990s war, the building suffered significant damage, and a lack of regular maintenance necessitated a comprehensive renovation project carried out between 2019 and 2020. Unfortunately, the renovation endeavour failed to preserve the building's original brick façade, possibly due to limited funding and the imposition of new thermal insulation standards.

Vedad Krkbešević

Philipp Meuser

Residential Building Papagajka

077 D

Hamdije Kreševljakovića nn
Mladen Gvozden, Dragan Bijedić
(Arhitekt firm)
1982

The building commonly known as Papagajka ('The Parrot Building') is a prominent example of a large-scale, five-storey postmodernist structure situated on the left bank of the Miljacka River. Its ground floor along with the underground levels are dedicated to commercial purposes, serving as offices, shops, and cafes, complemented by an underground garage. The upper floors are allocated for residential use, comprising apartments featuring both open and closed balconies. All of the apartments are accessed through an inner courtyard gallery – a feature that deviates from the conventional for the Sarajevan climate. The name 'Papagajka' originates from the building's distinctive façade colours: a combination of yellow and green hues that evoke the imagery of a tropical parrot. Moreover, an unexpected post-modernist element comes into view on the southern side of the structure, just a few metres from the foot of the hill on its south side: an imposing entrance characterised by a simplified Gothic style.

3

Philipp Meuser

Zvijezda's Skyscrapers

Čobanija 13
Ivan Štraus
1970s

078 D

Zvijezda's skyscrapers ('Star's Skyscrapers') are known as such due to a large advertisement for a commercial brand rather than for their star-like floor plan. They are characterised by their specific floor plan organised around a reinforced concrete core where the architect placed the main staircase with elevators – three identical volumes are organised radially around the centre core that host 18 storeys with six apartments on each level. Both skyscrapers have their own garage on the ground floor, providing additional open public space above them from which one enters the building. Their specific position in the urban matrix is characterised by their close proximity to the slopes of Mt. Trebević and lower-scale Old Town, which makes their appearance unexpected and as if they are leaning onto the mountain.

Vedad Krkbešević

Philipp Meuser

3

Svjetlost Office Building

079 **D**

Trg Oslobođenja
Halid Muhasilović
1976

The Svjetlost office building stands in the heterogeneous urban framework with Austro-Hungarian and modern representatives. Envisioned as a cornerstone for one of the rare urban squares of Sarajevo, Liberation Square, it responds both to the plasticity of the existing surroundings as well as forming its urban layout. The building defines its western façade by following the cornice height and roof slopes of its neighbours, with the bold material choices and the recessed base. Its volume, divided in two and playfully dispositioned, has two recessed floors instead of the usual one, allowing for a two-floor covered space on street level. This notion, in combination with the fragmented volume, was designed to move people towards the square. Although modernist, the façade is monumental in its expression, taking on the concepts of the Ljubljana architecture school of the

1960s, intending to resemble the patina of the surrounding buildings. A rigid vertical façade rhythm creates a contrast to the transparent base. In the crossover between the two is the accentuated primary structure, a defining element, also visible in the architect's other work, such as Skenderija. The building was designed to provide a pre-space, a gradual entrance to Liberation Square.

Ivan Štraus Archive

Residential Building Čobanija

080 D

Ejuba Ademovića 9
Haris Bradić, NB Atelier
2017

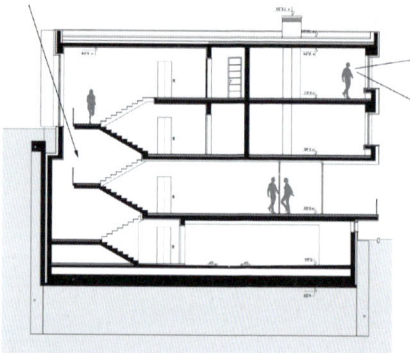

This project presents an interpolation into the existing urban structure on a steep terrain with the intention of not becoming obtrusive with its size or volume, while also tackling the significant technical challenges that such locations entail. The orientation of the existing slope to the north affected the arrangement of the walls and windows. The lower storey maintains the integrity of the main white volume, while the upper storey stands out for its continuous windows facing east, west, and north. Autochthonous stone known as Bradina was carved on-site and used to clad the ground level and northwest corner, giving the structure a valued layer of craftsmanship that sets it apart from its surroundings.

NB Atelier

Vakuf Hovadža Kemaludina

081 D

Ćemaluša 10
Reuf Kadić
1938–1939

The Vakuf Hovadža Kemaludina residential and commercial building represents one of the most significant avant-garde achievements of modernity from the period between the two world wars. Ferhadija Street was formed in the sixteenth century, with a mosque and a school on the site of the current buildings. A residential and commercial building was built on the site of the former school, while a complex residential and commercial building, popularly known as the 'JAT' skyscraper, was built on the site of the mosque. Functionally, the building is divided into the ground floor where there are business premises and the rest of the floors with a residential function. The façade of the building consists of several units: the ground part with the primary large, glazed areas of the business premises and the floor parts of the façades covered with green ceramics. The building features characteristic rows of large windows that provide good natural lighting in the interior spaces.

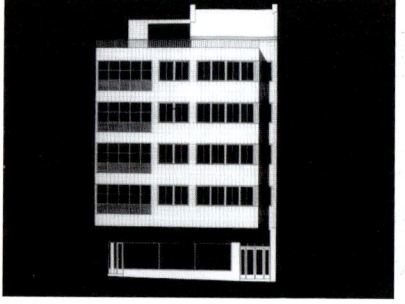

Emir Kadić Archive

Irhana Šehović

Four Residential Blocks in Branilaca Sarajeva

082 D

Branilaca Sarajeva nn
Reuf Kadić, Muhamed Kadić
1948

The architects of Sarajevo had an imperative task in the years following the Second World War: rebuilding the destroyed city. However, this important role came with significant challenges. There was a large influx of people into the capital in search of jobs and better homes in the rising post-war economy, and they had to be provided with dwellings. On the other hand, another result of the disastrous war events was the great poverty of the overall government. This dictated the funds reserved for the city reconstruction. During this period, the Kadić brothers worked together at the State Institute of Design and took it upon themselves to create the four large residential blocks in 'Branilaca Sarajeva' Street. Though restricted by regulations dictating maximum efficiency in space and fund usage, the architects managed to create projects that fit the area perfectly, while being able to house a lot of residents. The entry points are placed directly on the street but are inserted into the building's volume and are therefore provided protection. Some of the blocks contain roof terraces that are accessible and used by residents only. One of the city's many open markets also found its home in the courtyard of one of these blocks. This particular area holds many different object typologies from different time periods of the city's development and that makes these buildings invisible in a certain way. With their distinct small windows and loggias with their repetitive rhythm on façades deprived of any decorations, they serve as a homage to a time of rebuilding of society.

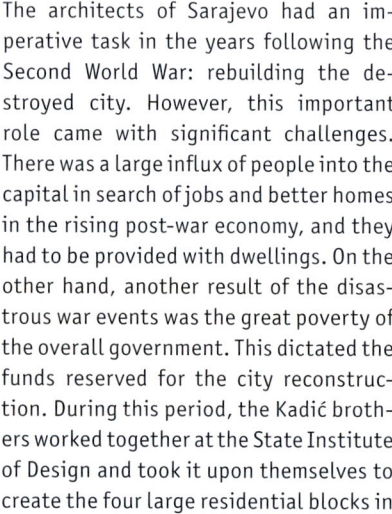

Timur Babić

Gajret

083 D

Branilaca Sarajeva 30
Dušan Smiljanić
1935

During Austro-Hungarian rule in Bosnia-Herzegovina, there were many cultural-societal societies in the country whose purpose was to help and educate the people. One of them was Gajret – a society founded in 1903 that promoted the education and culture of Bosniaks. The Gajret building in Sarajevo was built in 1935 based on the architectural design of Dušan Smiljanić. Horizontal rows of glass windows were

Obala Kulina Bana Residential Building

Obala Kulina bana 10
Jahiel Finci, Leon Kabiljo
1939

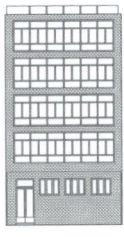

This somewhat concealed, tight-fitted building can very easily be overlooked in the cityscape. It was constructed during a period when new technologies had taken over, which resulted in the use of very common materials in new ways, such as glass as a dominant material and larger spanning constructions. This meant more light and space for the living quarters, which are, in the case of this building, the most dominant part of the floor plan and can very easily be spotted on the façade facing the street as the large windows. The rest of the area is divided into the sleeping and service quarters, all connected by a system of hallways positioned in the middle of the plan with a large central hall as the main communication point. This spatial configuration was dictated by the buildings elongated footprint in between existing structures, meaning that almost no natural lighting can be received from the sides. We can also see this on the façade facing the street, since the main entrance to the building is positioned on the left side.

3

Jeko Ono

realised on this building for the first time in Sarajevo. It has a rectangular floor plan with dimensions of 24.3 m × 14.9 m and a height to the ridge of 20 m, consisting of the ground floor, three storeys, and the attic. The building is covered with a gable roof. The composition of the façade is strictly symmetrical. The 4.1-metre-high ground floor and the rest of the building above it with clean surfaces broken by the central loggia on the first floor and the recessed surface of the staircase glass wall above, are different. In terms of construction and materials, the building has a reinforced concrete structure, a system of load-bearing walls, beams, and columns placed in the east-west direction. The external and internal load-bearing walls are filled with brick, and the façades are plastered, with the exception of the ground-floor part of the street façade, which is covered with polished granite. The Gajret building has been a national monument of Bosnia-Herzegovina and protected by the state since 2014.

Philipp Meuser

Bosnian Cultural Centre – (Grand Synagogue)

Branilaca Sarajeva 24
Rudolf Lubinsky, 1935
Ivan Štraus, 1964

085 D

During its construction, the Great Sephardic Temple, Sarajevo's largest synagogue, was designed to accommodate up to 2,000 worshippers. This remarkable structure built in the Pseudo-Moorish style by Rudolf Lubinski featured a striking elliptical copper cupola, making it the third largest synagogue in Europe at the time. The temple's dimensions measured 100 × 30 metres, providing ample space for approximately 1,000 visitors. The dome, a prominent feature of the building, rested upon 28 decorative concrete pillars, reflecting elements of the Maori aesthetic. Tragically, when Sarajevo was occupied during the Second World War, the temple

Bosnian Cultural Center Archive

3

and its adjacent buildings fell victim to demolition. However, the temple was later reconstructed and renovated in 1964 under the guidance of Ivan Štraus. The redesign incorporated a division into three horizontal levels, and an eye-catching stone menorah monument was erected in the portico. This statue, designed by Zlatko Ugljen, stands as a testament to the rich Jewish heritage spanning numerous centuries in Sarajevo. Since 1993, this historically significant building has served as the home of the Bosnian Cultural Centre (BKC). Within its premises, the BKC features a large auditorium, renowned for its exceptional acoustics, that can comfortably accommodate approximately 800 individuals. As a result, it has become one of Sarajevo's most sought-after venues for hosting a wide range of events, including concerts, film screenings, conferences, and other public gatherings.

Bosnian Cultural Center Archive

Irhana Šehović

Youth Theatre

086 D

Kulovića 8
Ahmed Hadžiosmanović
1977

The theatre building is hidden away between building blocks on Kulovića Street, not far from the National Theatre. This modernist gem is horizontal in composition and has a very simple cubic form with a vaulted extrusion that holds the theatre hall along with the main white prism, which has no windows on its western façade – the one facing the street. It is then placed on a pedestal of dark stone and glass that is the ground floor area and houses the main foyer and public areas for visitors as well as some workshops and ateliers. Following the two side staircases from the foyer, visitors emerge onto the first floor where the auditorium, with its red velvet seating, is placed into the centre of the floor plan, making

it symmetrical. The storage and dressing areas that flank the stage also help in establishing this order. Underneath all of this is a subterranean floor where staff offices are located. The main structure of the building is completed in reinforced concrete pillars, with the envelope constructed in hollow brick and then clad in stone. The vaulted ceiling of the auditorium helps in spanning the length and width of around 20 metres. Most of the building's final floor decorations are done in stone with occasional terrazzo and marine flooring.

Another one of the building's features is the Jurislav Korenić Cultural Square, which was opened to the public in 2018 after many years of serving as a car park. It was designed by Ahmet Prošić, a student of the Academy of Fine Arts Sarajevo, under the mentorship of professor Srđa Hrisafović and bears the name 'Via Vitae' ('The Way of Life').

Drawing: Amina Suljić

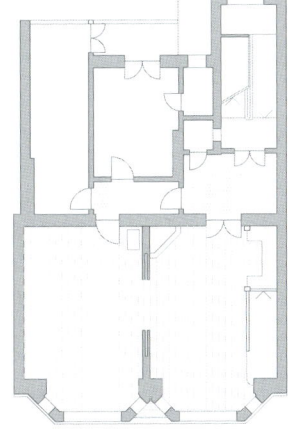

Haris Bulić

3

Damić House
Radićeva 10
Helen Baldasar, Dušan Smiljanić
1926–1927

087 D

Damić House, one of the first buildings to be constructed in the modern style in Sarajevo, was declared a national monument. The building holds most of its original appearance since it did not sustain significant damage during the war years. It was designed and constructed for the use of the Damić family, who lived and worked in the building. Positioned on an irregular rectangular site, the building closes an atrium with the large, main part and two smaller objects that held workstations. The main house consists of a ground floor, subterranean floor that follows the form of the building, two above ground floors, and an attic area. This is the part that is visible from the main street and holds the famous, symmetrical façade with its closed overhead balcony, and a small, triangular loggia. This unit housed the living and office areas of the building. The ground floor is broken at the right end by a passage that extends all the way to the courtyard and also holds the entrance to the building's residential hallway. The load-bearing structure of the building was achieved with reinforced concrete, the walls with brick, and the beams carrying the concrete slabs are wooden. The entire façade is decorated in coloured plaster. The interior of the building has gone through some minor adjustments to accommodate present-day living standards.

Drawing: Elša Turkušić

Almin Zrno

Josip Stadler
Priest Dormitory and Chapel
(Vrhbosna Archdiocese)
Josipa Štadlera 7-9
Nikola Maslej (author)
Adnan Pašić (redesign)
2007–2011

088 D

This building is located in the urban matrix from the period of Austro-Hungarian rule, which is a stylistic characteristic of most neighbouring buildings. The west side of the Priest's Home contains the building of the Catholic Seminary by architect Josip Vancaš, while the east side has a free-standing urban villa, also the work of Vancaš. The realisation represented the interpolation of the audience building between the urban villa and the Priest's House. The structure is divided vertically into three interconnected functional units: a garage with the accompanying facilities on the ground floor, first floor, and basement; a commercial space and multi-purpose hall on the second floor; and apartments with accompanying facilities on the third and fourth floors.

The upper volume is yellow as a continuation of the historic Priest's Home building, while the lower volume is clad in carefully chosen micrite limestone stone as a true dialogue with the walls of the nearby villa's courtyard. The gesture of separating the corner and the majority of the volume from the ground not only makes the garage entrance more convenient, but it also makes the overall building more inviting, improving the quality of public space. The constituent part of this complex is the Chapel, a modest square chamber with an altar and three benches with distinctive translucent panels depicting the Stations of the Cross. The pursuit of a meditative ambiance is an essential aspect of the interior design. Square and perpendicular extrusions in the ceiling and walls cast a variety of indirect colours into the space below, and their placement, dimensions, and hues are all chosen for their efficacy in illuminating various groups of the interior. Colourful lights reflect off of white walls and light maple wood furnishings to create a space that is both contemplative and spiritual.

Almin Zrno

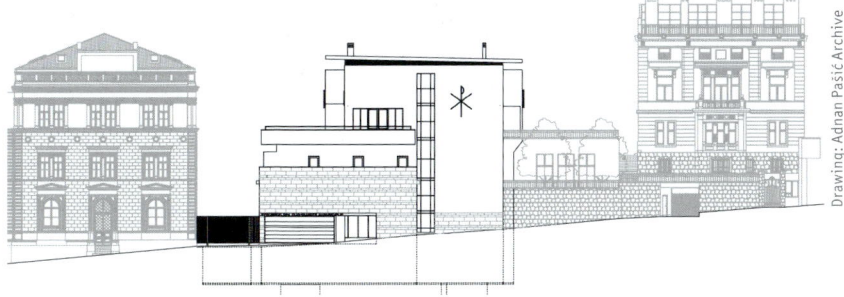

Drawing: Adnan Pašić Archive

Kaptol Residential Buildings 089 D

Kaptol nn
Ivan Štraus
1976

The Kaptol residential block occupies space in close proximity to the city centre but is positioned in a way that it has a memorable level of privacy. It was designed purely as a composition of residential volumes overlooking the city centre. The block hosts six buildings organised in two urban groups with an accompanying staircase that was redesigned in the 2010s. The two urban groups are organised as sets of three joined buildings with a labyrinth of pathways on different levels following the terrain's slope. Each building is designed as a four-storey yellow cube supported by four pillars connected with a cassetted reinforced concrete plate. This urban and architectural setup allowed the architect to focus the experience of these buildings on their amazing position on a sloped terrain that allows city views to all residential units.

3

Vedad Krkbešević

Dženat Dreković

Kaptol Stairs

Kaptol nn
Dina Šamić, Nermina Zagora,
Architectural studio Firma
2013

090 D

Due to its exceptional surroundings and location in the very centre of Sarajevo, the Kaptol Stairs have always occupied a special place in the hearts of the city's inhabitants. By changing the usual relationship between strictly functional and monumental urban elements, the main goal of the design team was to conceive this urban intervention as a completely new and distinctive urban space for Sarajevo. This was achieved by assigning additional cultural and educational qualities to the basic functional role of ordinary staircases. In this way, the newly designed 120 steps and seven landings have transformed Kaptol into a new meeting place for citizens, offering beautiful and unconventional views of the city. Each of the seven landings is devoted to a poet whose verses and a short biography are printed on the peripheral wall. The paving consists of two local stone types varying in colours and sizes, thereby creating the main movement in a very discreet and unpretentious way. The lighting was designed with equal sensitivity to the spirit of the place, discreetly emphasising each of the seven landings. The concept and final structure of the staircase elegantly fits into the existing urban tissue and in no way disrupts the current environment.

Musical Stairs

091 D

Pruščakova nn
Nermina Zagora, Dina Šamić,
Architectural studio Firma
2016

The existing public staircase in Pruščakova Street in a city core that connects two downhill and uphill parts of Sarajevo was part of a contemporary urban reconstruction effort. Besides its central location, the stairs are extremely important, as they provide an entrance landing to many residential and commercial objects. The key feature of the staircase is the 60-cm-wide and 70-m-long black stripe dancing and curving along the existing urban stairs, connecting the city centre with uphill residential neighbourhoods. Only after walking along the stripe does one see the most important part of this urban intervention – music boxes, or jukeboxes, each dedicated to a group or individual artist. Its bold appearance contrasts the stone pavement of the stairs and the concrete façades of the surrounding buildings, inviting the visitor to touch and interact with it.

Irfan Redžović

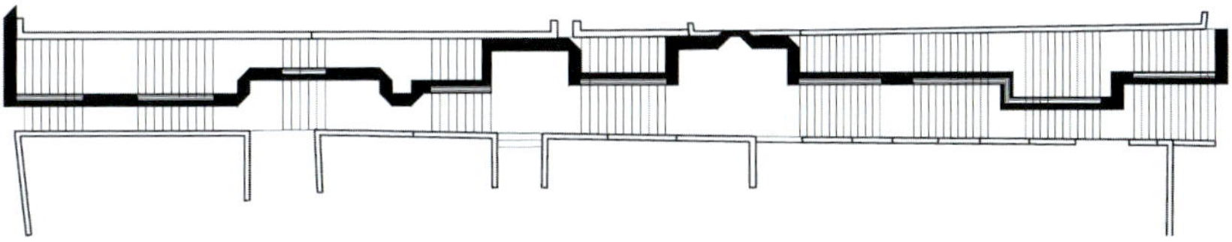

3

Irfan Redžović

Sun Housing Complex (Naselje Sunca)

Dalmatinska
Ivan Štraus
1972

Timur Babić

Architect Ivan Štraus has an anthology of specific forms with pure geometry and powerful proportions, with both inarguably part of his pioneering work on the Sun housing complex nestled on slopes of Mejtaš, an out of the ordinary and luxury neighbourhood. With modernist interpretations of terrace housing popping up all around Europe in the 1970s , Štraus' Sun is the first known instance of such a typology in Yugoslavia, with its importance undeniable in the Sarajevo mountainous context. The terraces follow the topography, as well as movement of the sun. In their rhythmic, layered composition, they reflect the philosophy of Bosnian oriental houses, mandating enough sunlight, a view towards the outside, as well as veiled areas, privacy, and garden spaces. The house concept is expanded vertically into units of up to four floors and densified. Its playful urban expression is further emphasised using bridges and terraces. The architect defined the scale as the only component of the existing surroundings upon which he based his expression in this work. The typology is created out of two distinct elements: a block system below and free-standing structures of residential villas scattered above – resonating a high-ambient-value Sarajevo amphitheatre with contemporary expression.

Archive Ivan Štraus

Timur Babić

Primary School
Silvije Strahimir Kranjčević
(Scouts' Hall)
Mehmed-paše Sokolovića 2
Juraj Neidhardt
1964

093 D

Originally built as a meeting place for the Scouts of Sarajevo and the entire Socialist Republic of BiH, the Scouts' Hall now serves a different purpose as the home of the public Primary School Silvije Strahimir Kranjčević. However, the history of the building has not been forgotten, and it still retains its significance in the city's architectural heritage. Despite being one of the last projects designed by the renowned architect Juraj Neidhardt, the Scouts' Hall is often overlooked by locals and visitors alike. Its unique features, such as the striking V-shaped columns and the small observatory dome, are a testament to the building's importance in Sarajevo's architectural landscape. While the observatory dome remains a dominant feature of the building's design, the large hall for events and accompanying rooms were also added to create a versatile space. However, the facility was not originally intended for use as an educational institution, and its layout and design are not ideal for modern-day school requirements. As a result, the school now has one of the lowest student populations in the city. Despite this, the Scouts' Hall continues to be an important piece of Sarajevo's architectural and cultural history.

3

Philipp Meuse

Amer Kapetanović

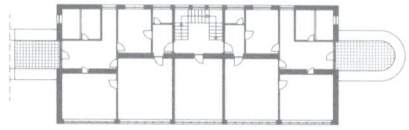

Džidžikovac
Residential Complex

Džidžikovac

Reuf Kadić, Muhamed Kadić
1947–1949

094 D

Immediately after the end of the Second World War, the rapid urbanisation of Bosnia and Herzegovina followed, and war-ravaged Sarajevo started to rebuild, both structurally and spiritually. As a result, the city was inhabited by a large number of residents from all parts of the country at the time. The city announced a competition called 'Dzidžikovac Colony' in 1947 and the proposal submitted by the Kadić brothers succeeded. The access to the buildings themselves is atypical, considering that the inhabitants of

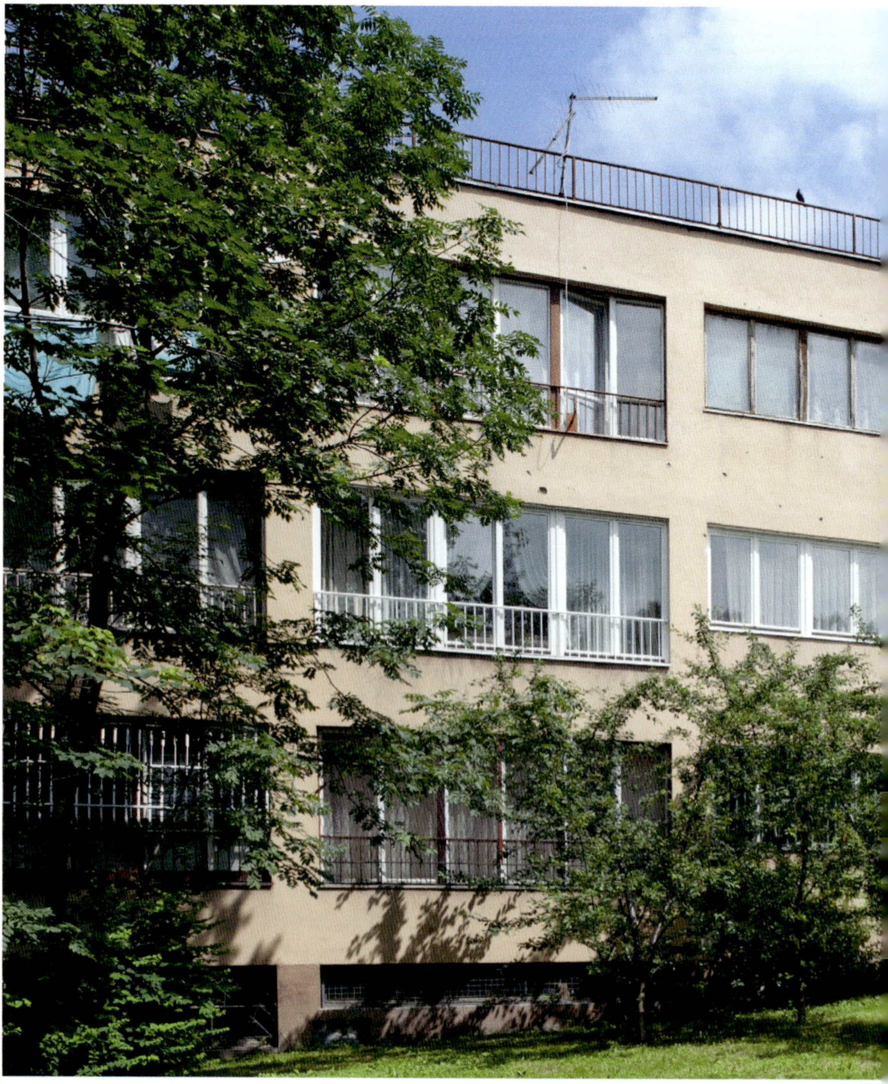

Sarajevo remember these houses for their narrow side or the street façades that were dominated by elliptical terraces full of greenery. The entire complex consists of eight three-storey buildings in three rows divided into individual units by designing large terraces between the two buildings for the users of both buildings. A passage was made possible under the terraces and thus a possible longitudinal barrier was opened. Between the rows of buildings there is a public green area with benches and playgrounds that have been maintained ever since the time of construction, but the small public swimming pool was removed many decades ago. The dynamic relationship between full and empty on the front of the buildings emphasises a synergistic combination of architecture and nature. The façade is dominated by large openings, unusual for construction in Sarajevo until then. Several public spaces were built, such as a shared flat roof and canopies on the ground floor, all with the aim of collectivising the population.

Archive Emir Kadić

Ervin Prašljvić

Čekaluša Residences

Čekaluša, Džidžikovac
Andrija Čičin Šain
1953

095 D

Andrija Čičin Šain had the very challenging task of incorporating contemporary residential architecture into the pre-existing local environment leaning against the already built mosque. With previous experience from the house in the town of Konjic, the author skilfully uses architectural tools based on Juraj Neidhardt's hypotheses. Čičin Šain built three residential buildings, two of which are cubic volumes with hipped roofs, while the third is a multi-apartment high-riser with a vertical tendency. The complex is enveloped by a semi-circular rustic stone wall that appears as a common thread of the project. The buildings at the intersection of the streets are particularly memorable, with a clear horizontal stereometry with a deep eaves roof.

Recessed balconies with a construction similar to the bondruk structure are undoubtedly associated with the local ambience. In this way, the author overcomes the transition from the already developed *mahala* spirit to a contemporary vertical volume as a continuation of the street row, without special ornaments or personal gestures. This spatial interaction of horizontal and vertical volumes, interweaving of residential and sacred, contemporary and traditional underlines the author's desire to develop a new society that does not neglect the local.

Ivan Štraus Archive

Zlatko Ugljen Archive

Libyan Consulate (Residency of the of Presidency of SR B&H)

096 D

Tahtali sokak 17
Zlatko Ugljen
1976–1978

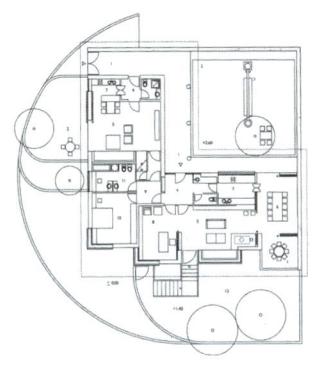

Located at the unusual intersection of three streets (Himzarina, Avde Sumbula, and Tahtali Sokak) and unlike others in the area, this building has a representative openness of its corner towards the north-west. The residency consists of three distinct formal elements: the basement hidden behind the curved wall defining the street, the main white volume shaped towards the corner, and the steep inhabited roof. The architect was led by the unwritten laws significant for the basic concept of the traditional houses in the area: 'successive gradation of courtyard, porch, house, and garden; mutual interpretation of open, semi-open, and enclosed indoor spaces; two-dimensional spaces separating the house from the outside world strictly respecting the intimacy of the home; and isolated courtyard as a buffer from and a direct link to the outside'. It is easy to notice the intention of organic embedding into the tissue of Sarajevan *mahala* while interpretating local architectural identity elements in a contemporary way in line with the approach of critical modernism.

3

Elementary School Musa Ćazim Ćatić

097 D

Čekaluša 53
Mate Baylon
1930

This school is one of the representative projects of architect Mate Baylon, one of the pioneers of Sarajevo and Yugoslavian modern architecture. It is based on some of the principles of the International Style: clean volumes and rectilinear forms; light, taut plane surfaces without any applied ornamentation or decoration; and open interior spaces with an inside-outside relationship. The main body of the school is composed of three repetitive vertical volumes facing the street, with its inside, south-facing component containing classrooms, creating a comb-like layout. In addition, the street is defined by the lower, rounded volume at the corner, making the building recognisable in the area.

Archive

Medical Centre of the University of Sarajevo

Grbavička nn
Rajko Mandić, Vedad Hamšić
1996

098 **D**

This Medical Centre of the University of Sarajevo campus holds several historical layers, starting from the Austro-Hungarian buildings that are still in use to extensions built during the Socialist period right through to new contemporary post-war buildings. After the damage inflicted to the campus during the Bosnian War of 1992 to 1995, a new project was commissioned for the design of the central building of the Medical Centre of the University of Sarajevo in 1996. It was built as a ten-storey facility hosting the main entrance followed by new surgical rooms, patient rooms, and other much needed capacity extensions. Compared to its Socialist-style neighbours, the new building was stripped of any unnecessary architectural communication and now appears as a gentle white stone giant overlooking the entire campus.

Traumatology Clinic

Bolnička 25
Branko Bulić
1984–1985

099 **D**

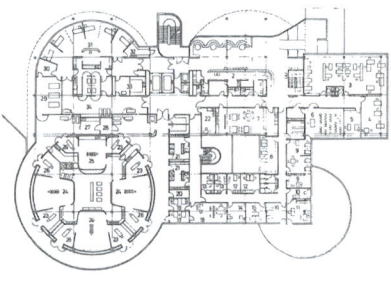

This clinic is part of the larger University of Sarajevo Clinical Centre complex, which is the largest hospital in the country. The complex was formed during the late nineteenth century and has been expanded and rebuilt over the years to the present. As the city's population grew and the Clinical Centre became the medical hub of the then Socialist Republic of Bosnia and Herzegovina, the need to create a well-designed Traumatology Clinic arose in the late 1970s. The specificity of the clinic lies in the form that follows very clear treatment procedures and facilitates fast administration. Upon completion of the construction, it also housed the Plastic (Reconstructive) Surgery Clinic. The unusual circular shapes are combined into a harmonised composition that allow for a one-way path of patients from reception and until release. To this day, the traumatology building is the main entry point for the majority of patients and their first encounter with the treatment system. Architect Ivan Štraus noted in one of his publications that: 'The architect paid great attention to the design aspect, trying to ensure that it is in harmony with the perfection of the function. The soft lines of the circular forms, their whiteness, and the quality of the execution are united into a unique plastic entity of high architectural value.' The project was awarded the republican Borba award for the most successful architectural achievement in Bosnia and Herzegovina in 1985. The building received a new façade through a project to increase energy efficiency in 2022, but a result of this was the loss of parts of its original finishing.

Philipp Meuser

Faculty of Architecture and Faculty of Civil Engineering

Patriotske lige 30
Jovan Korka, Emanuel Šamanek
1950s

100 D

The building was initially designed as the Technical faculty building and intended to house only two departments. However, they had developed into separate faculties, and there was not enough space for the equipment, so the Architecture and Civil Engineering faculties were placed here. The building's basic design was heavily influenced by the steep terrain, challenging geological conditions, and geomechanical constraints that made it extremely difficult to build. It is separated into two main units, both rectangular in shape with very dominant straight lines, and a horizontal composition: the classroom unit and the staff unit, with the addition of lecture halls. This division is present even today with a few minor changes where some staff offices have been mixed into the classroom area. The first unit with the classrooms is larger, as it is meant to be occupied by a large number of people, frequently moving in big groups. A long hallway cuts through the middle of the floor plan with classrooms, offices, and amenities on each side. At a certain point, there is a large, open staircase connecting the floors. Both the southern and northern façades are covered in large windows that allow enough daylight into all the classrooms as well as the stairway area. The second unit is much narrower, as it is not meant to be frequented by many people, but the layout is very similar to the first. A long hallway cuts through the middle of the floor and is flanked by offices on each side. This area, facing east and west, is also covered in windows, which is especially good for the library area that is placed here. The lecture halls, which are designed as additional volumes, can be accessed from this area. The main roof is done in vaulted sections, which is one of the most outstanding features of this building, but it also has a variety of accessible and inaccessible flat roofs. The building as well as the institution has undergone changes and renovations. The new library design that successfully promotes contemporary values through a transparent open plan and plenty of light becomes the new favourite place for architecture students to research and study.

3

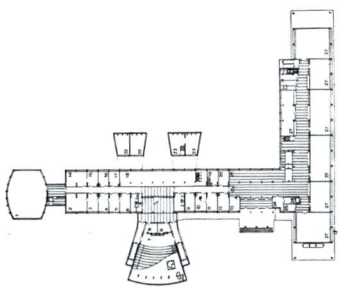

Design / Erdin Salihović

Breka Residential Complex

Jovana Bijelića, Ahmeta
Muratbegovića and others
*Hamdija Salihović, Bogdan
Božović, Momir Hrisafović*
1987–1989

101 D

The settlement of Breka was one of the last to be built before the turmoil of the war and still in the midst of the Olympic euphoria. It is located in the very far north of the Centar municipality, not far from the university Clinical Centre and with a southern orientation and a view of the city. It is another major urban-architectural undertaking designed and realised by the Institute of the Faculty of Architecture in Sarajevo headed by architects Hamdija Salihović, Bogdan Božović, and Momir Hrisafović. The project planned approximately 1,000 new apartments for around 3,500 residents in a block concept of one- to four-storey buildings around the perimeter of the settlement, while the central part was planned to include pedestrian streets. Within this project, a public-cultural content that was to be located next to the walkways in the central part of the location was also designed, but never realised, which only further argues that the ambitions in construction were often too great and the projects therefore remained unfinished. This public content included a library, multifunctional hall, craft centre, catering facilities, etc. The tendency of the architects was the concept of quiet housing, which was somewhat successful with the help of buried parking spaces. The specificity of this settlement is the irresistible similarity of the buildings, even though they are designed by three different authors. The basic features are the materialisation of the façade in yellow and

Hamdija Salihović

red brick, and the cantilevered mansard roofs at an angle of 75 degrees. In addition, the rulebook on technical measures and conditions for the thermal protection of buildings required the sandwich wall. The volume of the building itself is dynamically broken, so that there is no continuous line or tiresome façade repetition at all.

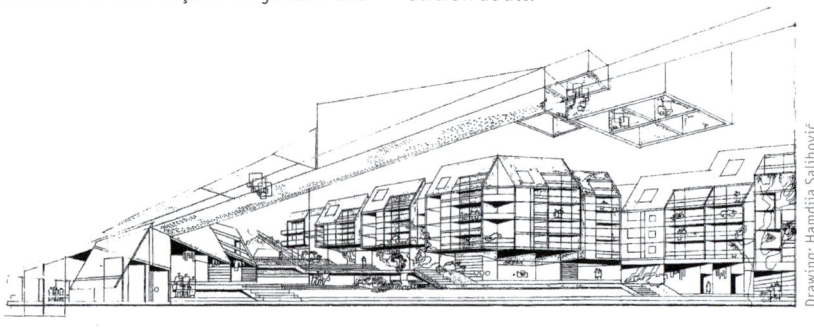

Drawing: Hamdija Salihović

3

The Parental House

102 B

Betanija nn, Jezero
*Normal arhitektura
(Adna Ahmedić, Armin
Sadiković, Dino Eminagić,
Ermin Hadžić, Emir Salkić,
Muhamed Serdarević, Tarik Musakadić)*
2013–2016

The Parental House consists of ten apartments spread over three levels and a ground floor that is connected to the surrounding public space and contains the kitchen, dining room, and other spaces. The underground level features a small conference room and other auxiliary spaces for educational workshops. The exterior of the building is all white, while the interiors of the apartments, designed by ten different architecture practices, are brightly coloured and spread across the three levels on the southern side to offer varying views of the surroundings. A 'cut' on the north side, designed to resemble a waterfall, breaks up the uniformity of the closed façade and connects all three levels of the building to the rooftop terrace, allowing light to

Eldin Hasanagić

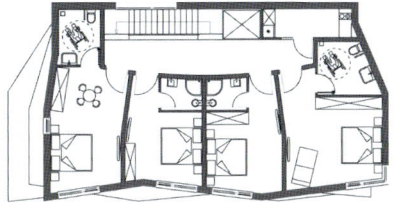

reach the interior walkways. The rooftop terrace, which was created by local residents and friends of the project, can be accessed through these walkways.

ZETRA Olympic Complex and Olympic Hall

Alipašina nn

Dušan Đapa, Lidumil Alikalfić,
1978–1982

103 B

The Zetra Olympic complex is the largest sports complex in Bosnia and Herzegovina and was designed for the XIV Olympic Games held in Sarajevo in 1984. Zetra stands for *zelena transverzala* in Bosnian ('green transversal'). It is located on a plot bounded from the north by Koševo Stadium, to the east by auxiliary football pitches and the cemetery of St. Josip, and to the west along Alipašina Street, and it covers an area of over 7 hectares. Its powerful roof structure made of steel pipes covers a space the size of a football pitch for 2,500 spectators. In addition to such large dimensions, the hall has balanced spatial relationships, which affects viewers' feeling of comfort, regardless of their place of observation in the auditorium. The complex includes the following facilities: 1. Olympic Hall; 2. Speed Skating Stadium, 3. Boiler room; 4. Annex of the Olympic Hall; 5. City heating plant, 6. Car parks and service road; 7. Parks and green areas. The Olympic Hall is a multi-storey building. The ground floor has changing rooms with bathrooms, small halls (3), a shooting range, a bowling alley, a fitness centre, a ballroom, bathrooms for the audience, storage, and corridors for gathering athletes. The large hall is in the basement (105 × 100 m) along with a fighting area of 100 × 60 m, and the assembly-disassembly ice area of 30 × 60 m. There are six entrances for visitors as well as gallery spaces. There is an audience hall with a bar on the first floor to the west of the hall. The main hall was designed and built as a multi-purpose hall, satisfying all the requirements of international sports federations for indoor sports. With such a design procedure, the hall could be permanently used for sports and recreation. The external appearance of the hall under the corrugated copper cover does not give any impression of the spaciousness and size of its interior. The architects of ZETRA received the Borba award for the most successful architectural achievement in Yugoslavia in 1983.

Ivan Štraus Archive

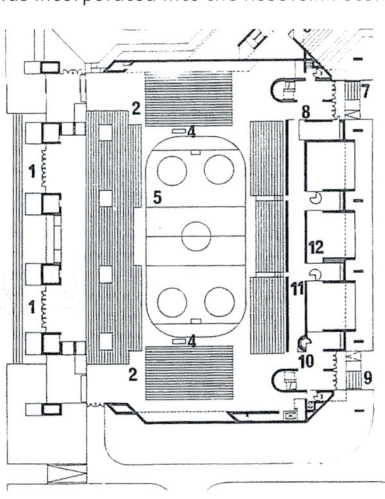

Asim Ferhatović Hase Stadium   104 B

Patriotske lige 35
*Vaso Todorović, Anatolij Kirjakov
(initial design)* 1950
*Lidumil Alikalfić, Dušan Đapa
(reconstruction, addition)* 1984

Formerly known as Koševo Stadium, this stadium was built and opened in 1950 according to a design by Vaso Todorović and Anatolij Kirjakov. Construction of the Koševo Stadium began in 1947. Utilising the natural amphitheatre, the stadium was incorporated into the Koševski Potok valley and possesses the characteristics of a landscape stadium. In 1950, work commenced on installing the athletic track and constructing retaining walls to enable the expansion of the stands, giving the stadium its initial elliptical contours. As part of the preparations for the organisation of the XIV Winter Olympic Games, a complete reconstruction of the stadium began. According to the project, the western stand was transformed into the central stand, while the rest was demolished and replaced with new stands, giving it a fully elliptical shape. After the opening of the Olympic Games, it officially gained the status of an Olympic stadium. During the aggression against Bosnia and Herzegovina, the stadium suffered significant damage, resulting in reduced seating capacity. However, the stadium retained its distinctive characteristic seat colour, which is not associated with any particular city club or the national team, but together with the sloping seats that follow the terrain configuration, it blends the constructed structure into the context. In a broader urban context, its colour and rounded form seek to maintain continuity with the aforementioned green axis.

3

Damir Begović

Bosnalijek Headquarters
Jukićeva 53
Hasan Ćemalović
2012

This building originated as a reconstruction of an existing warehouse structure. The goal was to create a representative facility for an important pharmaceutical company to house the company's management and part of the quality control laboratories. To maximise the usable space in this deep building, a lightwell was designed to penetrate through the structure, providing natural light to the office spaces in the administrative area. The building has two separate entrances – one for employees and another service entrance for the kitchen and associated storage areas. In addition to a restaurant, the building also features a conference hall. The façade of the building was executed in a contemporary design with a clear alternation of solid and void elements. The use of double-glazed panels facilitated the final layout of the floor plan, allowing for the neutralisation of various openings on the building's façade. A dynamic line with horizontal tendencies, along with curved endings and the use of modern materials completely masked the original purpose of the building while emphasising the business tendencies of the company under whose auspices this building was created.

Damir Begović

Hum – Television and Radio Tower

Put za Hum
1982

Illustration: Molimao, Sandin Mededović

Hum Hill, rising 812 metres above sea level and located in the northern central area of the Miljacka valley, can technically be considered a mountain due to its height. The city of Sarajevo strategically selected this location to house its main TV and radio signal relay tower, owing to its position and importance. The initial construction took place in the 1960s, but the tower we see today, reaching a height of 78.5 metres, was erected in the early 1980s. The tower is a structure composed of steel and concrete, resembling a 'needle' piercing through a 'bubble'. The 'needle' portion consists of a reinforced concrete core with an antenna at its tip, while the 'bubble' is made of steel and plexiglass, housing technical rooms across four floors. The base of the tower is encompassed by several smaller additions designed accordingly. The recent undertaking of the Hum Park-Forest project aims to provide the citizens of Sarajevo with additional recreational zones. Consequently, a significant area of the hill has been preserved. This initiative involves the creation of new walking routes, pathways, improved public transport, and better connectivity to the city centre. Additionally, it includes the reconstruction of the tower, which suffered extensive damage during the 1990s war and the Siege of Sarajevo. Despite the damage, it still functions as the most crucial TV and radio signal relay station in the country.

3

Sabina Hodović

3

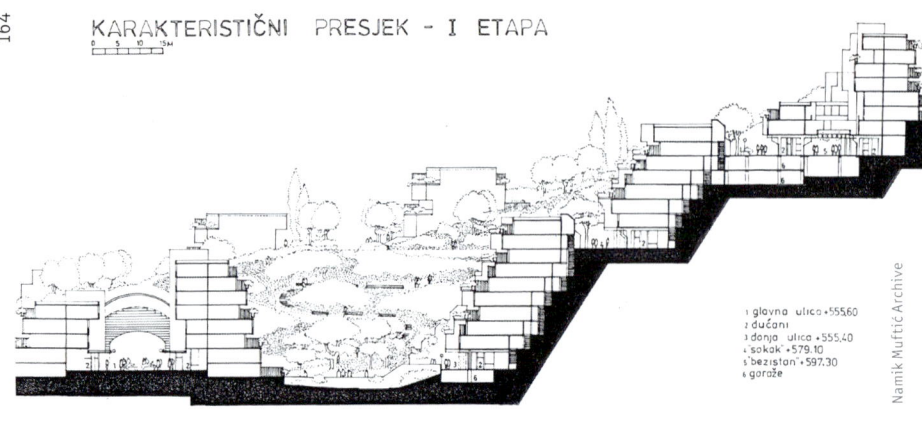

1 glavna ulica +555,60
2 dućani
3 donja ulica +555,40
4 'sokak' +579,10
5 'bezistan' +597,30
6 garaže

Ciglane Residential Complex 107 C

Merhemića Trg, Husrefa Redžića,
Avde Hume, Hakije Kulenovića
Namik Muftić, Radovan Delalle
1976–1989

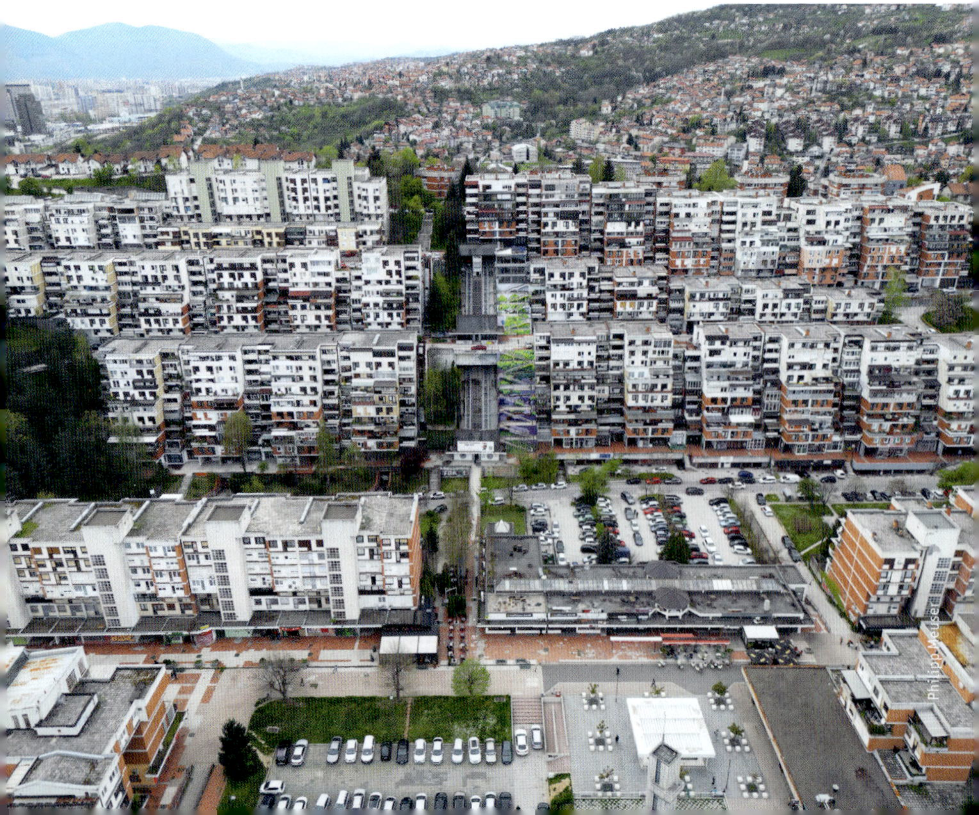

The brick factory that gave the whole area its name (literally 'Brickhood') opened in 1879 on the location of what is now the Ciglane residential complex. Almost a hundred years later in 1965, the Sarajevo city planning institute made a general urban plan for this area, the first of its kind in former Yugoslavia, suggesting the construction of a contemporary residential neighbourhood. Following the plan, a public call was announced in 1974, and among 57 ideas, the winners were Namik Muftić and Radovan Delalle. The Ciglane complex has a gross surface area of 146,390 m² and 1,451 residential units located on a total area of 15.86 ha. The neighbourhood also has a complete system of pedestrian and car lanes, squares, and many additional services. Ciglane has a density of 373 residents per hectare. During the design and construction process, the authors developed the term 'urbarchitecture' that represents a specific megastructure of continuous volumes, designed according to place and time, at the same time allowing the users to be

involved in the design process. Urban-spatial characteristics provided the construction of a neighbourhood inspired by traditional residential structures on the Sarajevo hills. The goal was to form different micro ambiences with sights on Mt. Trebević, where a very important aspect was flexibility, especially on hillsides where larger structural spans were used. The authors gave advice to residents on how to correctly use open spaces in which everyone has an open space and a view. Every apartment at the hillside has a terrace in front of the living room and in front of the bedroom. Until 1992 the flexibility and adapting of the open spaces to residents' needs were regulated by the authorities, resulting in amazing ideas by users, while in the post-war era, more than the last proportion of interventions were made illegally. Besides small private interventions on terraces, the complete residential complex has preserved its original form and function, with the additional construction of a mosque and a reconstruction of a public square. This systematic development can be labelled as 'unfinished' like many others from that era that dealt with new social arrangements. Instead of a fully developed metabolistic architectural dialect, it evolved into a mosaic of socially diverse tastes.

Pizzeria Fratelli

108 C

Merhemića Trg
Nedžad Hrelja,
Jasmina Hadžimešić, Emir Hasečić
2000

This 40-square-metre infill is installed in one of the Ciglane complex's passageways. The warm wood tones and sensual curvature of its wooden façade create an interesting focal point in an otherwise ordinary brick-and-mortar setting. The façade shields visitors from the gaze of passers-by during the day and at night allows for a symbolic extension of warmth and atmosphere into the immediate surroundings – the passage that would otherwise remain dark, unlit, and cold. It emphasises the idea of the passage with its length and entrances at both ends, and, despite occupying public space, it significantly improves its quality.

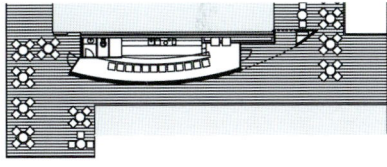

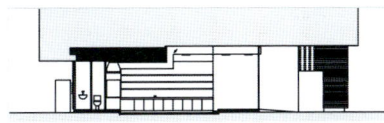

Nedžad Hrelja

Alipašina Residential Complex

Alipašina 17
Juraj Neidhardt
1947–1952

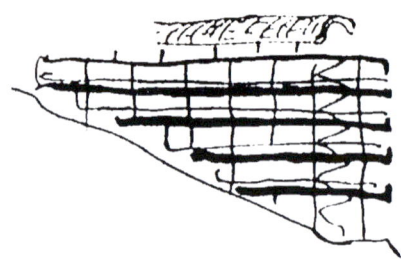

The consequences of the destruction of the Second World War were still being felt in the 1960s, so residential architecture maintained the aspiration towards building as many apartments as possible with modest investment. In such a context, Neidhardt designed two residential buildings on a street that was very busy due to its connection with the primary entrance to the city. The buildings are placed orthogonally toward the slope, which underlines the author's desire for the penetration of greenery into the space in between. Contrary to the previous practice of placing buildings linearly along the street, this spatial gesture dissolved the blocks and established the necessary green breaks that provoked better orientation of the apartments, ventilation, insolation, and movement through the neighbourhood. The buildings contain recognisable elements of regionalism, such as a solid stone base,

Philipp Meuser

a four-storey *doksat*, streets paved with cobblestones, and perforations on the façade of the building. The positioning of the volumes above the street develops an architectural dialect essential for the future of the Sarajevo school of architecture, which clearly emphasises the entrance sequences while at the same time covering the access to the buildings. Although some design elements and the author's writing refer to regional architecture, this project certainly contains elements of modernity in the context of volumes placed on pillars in the manner of Le Corbusier's buildings, with a very clear social tendency for the development of collective housing through common rooms, shared walkable roofs, and green areas between buildings.

Pasha Oko

Railway-Savings Fund Building

110 C

Augusta Brauna 4
Isidor Rajs
1938

3

The city's first skyscraper was constructed under the influence of modern architecture. The building is marked by its dominant straight lines where the verticality is dominant and emphasised through a column of windows on the western and eastern façades, while the northern and southern ones are broken by horizontal rows. The straight angles are contrasted in the area of the first floor with a white-coloured extrusion that overhangs the street with its semicircular finish. It is then held up by four load-bearing pillars clad in stone that also house one of the building's access points to the office areas. The finish of the tower is done in green plaster. Continuing down the street onto the western side, there is a smaller residential building with the height of a ground floor and two floors and it is directly connected to the tower through the inside as well. The entire tower has intertwining residential and office functions, making the plan of the building very complex. The apartments can be accessed from the third to eighth floors, with three residential units per floor. The first floors and the last ninth floor are reserved for office areas.

Residential Zone Crni Vrh

111 C

Kalemova , Tešanjska,
Nazečića, Kranjčevićeva
Mate Bajlon, Franjo Lavrenčić,
Bruno Tartalja, Stjepan Planić,
Danilo Kocijan, Franc Novak,
Dušan Smiljanić
1933–1939

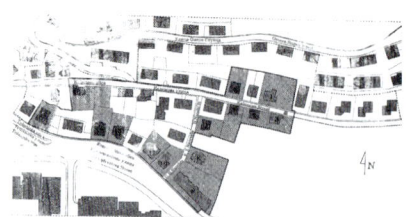

Pasha Oko

This residential zone is unique in Sarajevo as one of the only ones planned in the period between the two world wars and as a certain milestone in the rise of modern architecture and planning in the city. The initial master plan for Crni Vrh parcelled the site into 93 building plots on the larger area of the hill with a steep terrain configuration towards the south. It was financed by the Railway Workers' Loans and Aid Cooperative with the aim of alleviating social deprivation among railway workers. Some of the buildings along the streets of Kalemova, Kranjčevićeva, Tešanjska, and Halida Nazečića – about 14 detached houses and two buildings – have been listed as a national monument as the 'architectural ensemble of the Crni Vrh development' by the Commission to Preserve National Monuments of Bosnia and Herzegovina. All were designed in the period between the two world wars by leading representatives of the modern movement in the Kingdom of Yugoslavia. In 1933, an international architectural competition for housing typologies received 45 projects submitted from Sarajevo, Zagreb, Ljubljana, Belgrade, Split, and also from Prague, Paris, and Vienna.

The jury, including Sarajevo architects Dusan Smiljanic and Mate Bajlon, evaluated that none had completely fulfilled the task, and all awards were presented except first prize. Several works were inspired by the solutions of the Weissenhof Estate in Stuttgart and the Baba settlements in Prague. Documentation about the authors of individual buildings and the project phase is scarce. However, it is interesting that although the typological construction was originally conceived, all projects were designed and built as unique. It is generally assumed that the architects of this residential zone were heavily influenced by European tendencies and international style in terms of rational parcelisation and proportions between public and private zones, while also incorporating traditional unwritten rules

Irfan Salihagić

Farah Zubović

of Sarajevan' *mahalas* in terms of organic links between green zones and houses and the 'right to the view and insolation', a term coined 20 years later by Juraj Neidhardt and Dušan Grabrijan in the book *Architecture of Bosnia and the Way Towards Modernity*. The common reference to this modernist development is the Weissenhof Estate in Stuttgart, primarily because of the architectural language of modern and planning principles. However, it did not have the purpose of the exhibition per se. While many other buildings in the zone have experienced changes and reconstructions, the most representative and original is Villa Corn. There has been an initiative to reconstruct and create a Museum of Modern Architecture in Villa Corn, while there have also been inclinations to demolish and replace it.

General Hospital (Military Hospital)

Kranjčevićeva 12
Unknown architect
1976–1979

112 C

The General Hospital (Military Hospital) is the city's oldest medical facility. In 1962, a public architectural competition for the new building was held, and two second prizes were awarded, but no project was selected as the winning design to be built. More than a decade later, the JNA (Yugoslav People's Army) fostered a project that was eventually constructed. The building is located at the bottom of Crni Vrh Hill next to Marijin Dvor and Hastahana Park. The primary medical and surgical facilities, along with the required beds, are situated in the tower at the centre of the complex. The rest of the complex consists of lower buildings that house various facilities. The white rectangular tower façade is adorned with a rational repetition of south-facing windows and vertically adorned with slender strips that serve as both sunscreens and contribute to the building's overall aesthetics. At first glance, the General Hospital's tower appears to have nine storeys. However, the applied façade design conceals an additional five levels towards the ground. Through the clever implementation of a horizontal fluted façade strip on its first few floors, the perception of the building's actual scale is subtly altered.

3

Irhana Šehović

O2 Residential Complex

Zagrebačka nn, Kovačići
Hamdija Salihović
1972-1980

113 C

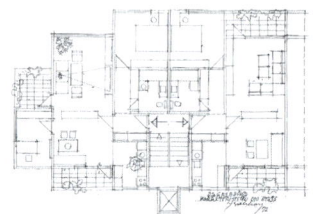

Drawing: Salihović Archive

The O2 urban-architectural project in Kovačići, which included the area from Vrbanja Bridge (Suada and Olga Bridge) to the Faculty of Agriculture, was developed in stages over an eight-year period. This residential complex consists of three buildings and public spaces, located between the river and an important road. At the time, this project was new and different from other urban and residential projects in Sarajevo. The main specificity was its composition and withdrawal from the road, the creation of a square facing the road, and a green zone facing the river. Even though the slightly broken volumes look random at first glance, they result from the relationship between two existing urban axes – the river and the road.

They form a dynamic composition with various views and walking possibilities. The design of the passages and a square with an underground parking garage and public shelter was given special consideration. All ground-floor units are commercial, and today they consist of different shops, cafes, and services. Aside from the location's general advantages, such as closeness to significant national institutions, the commercial zone, and public transport, the relationship of buildings to an open space must have contributed to this complex becoming one of the most desirable in the city.

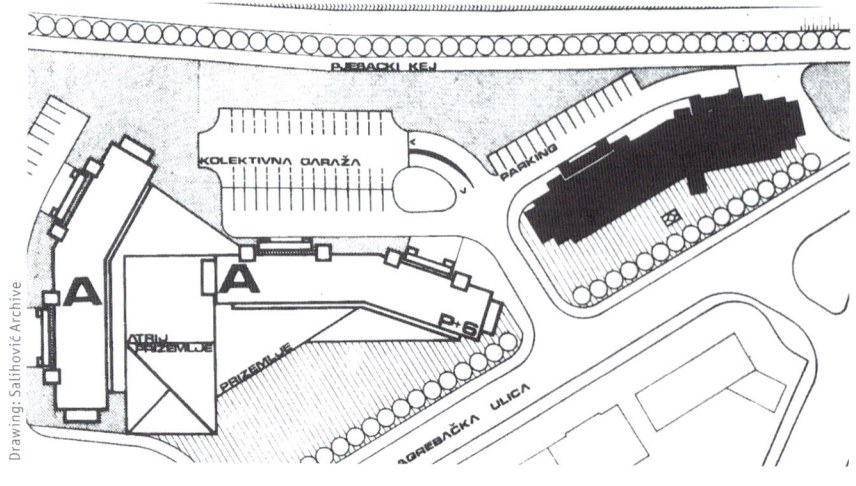

Drawing: Salihović Archive

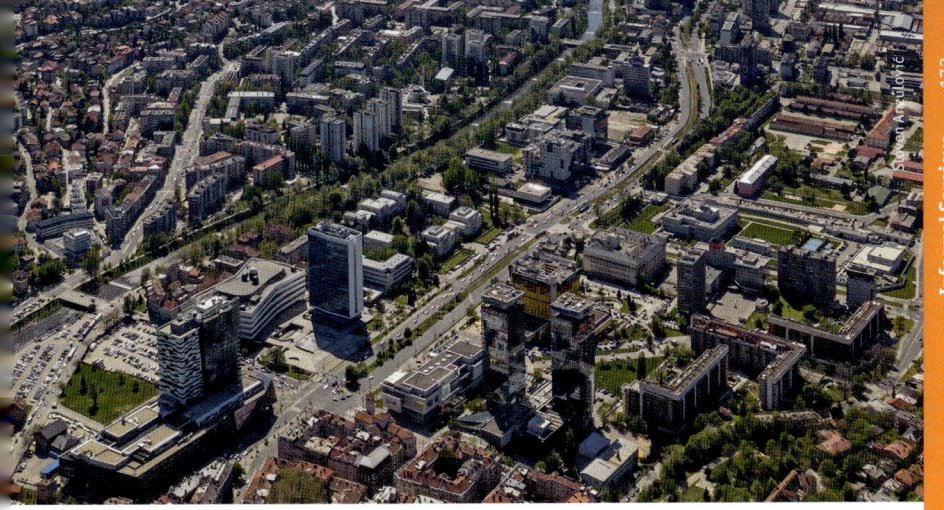

Kranjčevićeva Residential Buildings Complex

114 **C**

Kranjčevićeva, Franca Lehara
Mladen Gvozden
1985

This complex is located within the vibrant Marijin Dvor neighbourhood in close proximity to renowned landmarks such as the Hotel Holiday Inn and Unitic Towers. It also offers convenient access to the Alta shopping centre and the Railway Station. Enclosed by picturesque Kranjčevićeva Street and adjacent to the scenic Crni Vrh Residential Zone on one side and the notable Franca Lehara Street on the other, it is known for its distinctive urban planning. The axis of Franca Lehara Street originates from the Railway Station and culminates with captivating vistas of Mt. Trebević. Comprising three residential buildings shaped like an 'L', with varying side lengths, the structures are elevated above a foundation that accommodates commercial spaces, car parks, and a plethora of inviting public areas in between. Apart from its extensive use of brick, it has a distinctive top end facing Kranjčevićeva, with a slender one-storey white beam on one side and a concealed sloping roof with terraces on the other towards the south. This development represents the largest planned housing in the Marijin Dvor neighbourhood, encompassing a total net area surpassing 11,000 square metres. Thanks to its thoughtfully designed apartment layouts and public spaces, it is one of the most coveted residential destinations in central Sarajevo.

Aparthotel Centar

Muamera Omerbegovića 14
Sabrija Bilalić,
BP Projekt
2016–2019

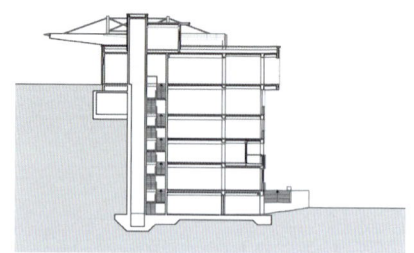

Michel I Wolf

This building juts out over the edge of a hill in a recently developed neighbourhood south-west of the Cultural and Sports Centre Skenderija, and it faces the transit road that circles the city centre. It acts as a link between two quite different parts of town due to the almost 15-metre height difference between its two sides. The building's two distinct façades are the result of its unique section and a typical programmatic mixture of aparthotel towards the slope side with views towards the city and on the other side towards a high traffic road and a petrol station. The one facing the city is made up of a series of smaller volumes that are cantilevered off the main volume and supported by accentuated red structural elements.

Children's House Grbavica ↓

Grbavička nn
Stari Grad Mostar and
i.d.e..a. Sarajevo
2019

This building was formerly the Boško Buha Youth and Culture Centre built in 1963 and named after a national war hero from the Second World War. It was famous for many generations of children before the war in the 1990s when it was completely destroyed. This new institution was envisioned as an educational and cultural centre with multipurpose spaces for a cinema, theatre, and workshops for the local community and children. The modest design features only an accentuated upper, slightly cantilevered volume with repetitive slats. Its position in the neighbourhood's urban matrix makes it one of the most important public meeting points.

Jasmin Braut

St. Ignatius of Loyola
Church and Pastoral Centre →

Ante Fijamenga nn
Novi Dom (Juro Pranjić,
Ana Bosankić)
2013–2019

After an intensive search spanning numerous years, the Society of Jesus acquired the only obtainable location for their parish in the Grbavica settlement. The site posed significant limitations in terms of both its location and size due to its proximity to Grbavica Stadium and sports hall, as well as being surrounded by densely populated individual houses. As a result, an inward-focused architectural style was employed, effectively encompassing the entire plot. The design prioritised an internal, enclosed atrium, which not only ensured tranquillity and respect for the occupants but also shielded them from external disturbances, serving as a preparatory space before entering the church. Through the use of white Brač marble cladding, the architects successfully accomplished their objective of making the church more visually distinctive within the existing surroundings. The church's symbolism is clearly

Shopping Centre Grbavica and 3 Residential Towers

118 B

Hasana Brkića nn
Ivan Štraus
1975

Michael Walczak

This urban design was created as part of a larger urban strategy to develop smaller-scale mixed-use neighbourhood centres. It consists of three 20-storey residential towers and a horizontal volume with numerous public-focused facilities, such as shops and cafes, a public underground garage, and a maze of pathways organised in several levels and interconnected by staircases and ramps. The horizontal volume, known simply as 'Shopping', is distinguished by its decorative concrete modular façade elements. The accompanying residential towers were designed to provide maximum insulation to all residential units by following the movement of the sun. Decorative concrete elements were placed at the towers' upper corners to emphasise their verticality while maintaining the spatial functionality of all apartments. The bold use of yellow is characteristic for architect Ivas Štraus, as several of his buildings in Sarajevo were finished in the same hue.

3

Katolički tjednik

articulated through its unique and well-defined silhouette, consisting of three gradually ascending volumes, culminating in an unassuming bell tower located at the most prominent corner facing the stadium and the Grbavica neighbourhood. This design strives to establish the church as a prominent and recognisable religious edifice in Sarajevo.

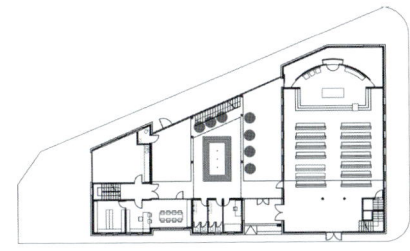

Ambulance Service

119 B

Kolodvorska 14
Mira Besarović
1970s

The Ambulance Service building is hard to miss and it is hard not to understand its purpose. The combination of red and white on its façade easily communicates its function, and its size follows; this two-storey building was made to be compact and efficient. Additional space in the underground area is used as service rooms following the fall in terrain of 4 metres. The architect snatched this opportunity and designed the base of the building and added a cantilever first floor for the administration offices.

Umihana Čuvidina
Elementary School Sports Hall

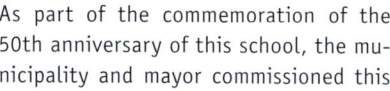

120 C

Smaila Šikala 1
Zijo Krvavac, Sakib Oković,
Dejan Tadić
(Architecture studio i.d.e..a.)
2021

As part of the commemoration of the 50th anniversary of this school, the municipality and mayor commissioned this sports hall project to expand the capacity of the school as well as to provide new contemporary facilities for sport education. The main aim of the project was to create a space that will develop into a primary educational, sports, and health centre in the Sarajevo neighbourhood of Boljakov Potok, which acts as a gravitational centre for over 10,000 people. The sports hall was built to Olympic standards and can accommodate up to 500 spectators, with an additional programme of a kindergarten space for 120 children, additional school facilities, 11 classrooms, a library, a school ambulance, a fitness centre, an underground car park with 40 space. Its southern façade is designed as a masked façade with thin perforated steel plates in four colours, according to the authors, inspired by the pack of colouring pens the architects frequently use for their concept drawings and sketches.

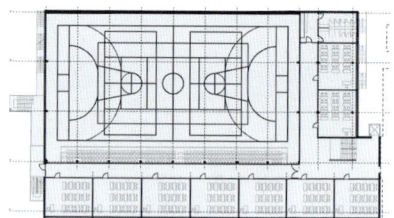

Dunja Krvavac

Sarajevo Waves Residential Building

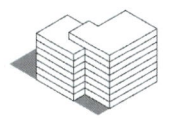

Barska 59
AHAKNAP+SAAHA
(Adnan Harambašić, Kenan Brčkalija)
2016

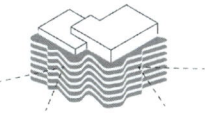

This project is the first phase of a larger housing development in Otes, a Sarajevo suburb with mountains and a river as its immediate and distant surroundings. The wave-like structure is added to the rationally rectangular building volume starting on the second floor in order to increase the interior space and create an in-between zone, while the exterior of the building is kept simple with white plaster and metal screens providing additional visibility protection to the apartment terraces. The interior façade of the building is covered in warm wooden ribs. This gives each unit a distinctive outdoor terrace, which becomes a defining architectural element.

Anida Krečo

Music Farm

Karla Malya bb, Ilidža
normal arhitektura (Emir Salkić, Muhamed Serdarević, Armin Mešić)
2008–2009

normal arhitektura

The Music Farm comprises a music studio and a house within a single architectural structure. The design embraces modern technology and production methods, blurring the line between industrial and office buildings. Located in a peaceful, green suburb called Ilidža, the building occupies the same size and footprint as its predecessor, with one side connected to a third existing structure. The structure features a sleek, sheet metal exterior with a pent roof, combining high-tech and traditional elements. The placement, quantity, and size of the openings, matching the façade's colour, indicate the interior layout: a closed grey cube for the two-storey studio and an open-plan brown cube for the three-storey house. The unevenly spaced, brown-rendered concrete frames, purely decorative in nature, add dynamism to the façade and emphasise the building's 'archetypal' form.

Jeko Ono

K67 Kiosk

123 D

Zaima Šarca nn / others
Saša Mächtig
1967–

For half a century, the iconic K67 kiosk –
a newspaper stand, lottery terminal, fast-
food restaurant, and copy shop – was an
integral piece of Sarajevo. The K67 kiosk
was designed and produced in 1968 in the
former Yugoslav Slovenia. Its lightweight,
compact design was based on polyfibre-
reinforced modules, and it was widely sold not only to countries in Eastern
Europe and the former Yugoslavia, but also to Japan and New Zealand. Although
the K67 design was based on the abili-
ty to combine numerous individual units
and can be expanded virtually indefinite-
ly with the option of different colours,
the single and double units in the colour
red were the most popular in Sarajevo.
It was added to the New York Museum of
Modern Art's collection of twentieth-
century design, and it gained even more
popularity after the museum's exhibition
on Yugoslavian architecture. As a valuable design, samples can be found in cities such as Berlin, Zurich, Vienna, among
others, and one has been restored and
displayed in Times Square in New York.
Meanwhile, it retains its ordinariness in
Sarajevo and is mostly reserved for fast-
food eateries.

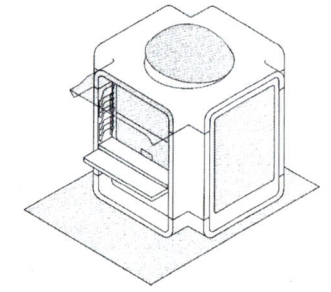

IMGRAD Ljutomer

Michael Walczak

Communello Trans

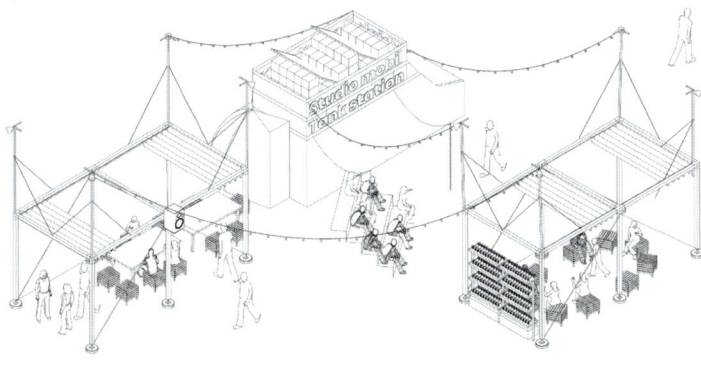

studio mobil/ think tank station

Vrazova 3
ETH Zurich, Urbanthinktank_next
(Hubert Klumpner and Michael Walczak)
2021–Ongoing

124 D

The studio mobil/think tank station is imagining a visionary city outdoor-laboratory, engaging ideas around the future of Sarajevo. By touring the city, taking to the streets, and performing sessions with partners, the station acts as a nomadic outdoor agora. As an alternative form of urban practice, the think tank station welcomes people to participate by (re)activating, collecting, and sharing knowledge about Sarajevo. It presents workshops, debates, and lectures around alternative urbanisation and urban spaces as the emerging theme that concerns all of us. Based on the idea of a gasoline station for the post-fossil fuel age – perhaps one of the most iconic twentieth-century purpose-built infrastructures – studio mobil/think tank station provides 24/7 services and infrastructure, including shelter, light, a library, performances, informal encounters, a market, and a continuous supply of food for thought, but without the gasoline – in short, a large-scale mobile sculpture anchored in public space. The studio mobil is connecting and bridging the global, regional, and local and is made accessible through a digital platform, developing a creative common framework of shared tools, knowledge, and projects.

3

Michael Walczak

Adnan Bubalo, Trebevic.ba

Trebević Viewpoint

Hrvatin nn, Mt. Trebević
Studio Arh (Kenan Zvizdić,
Merima Terović, Dino Sofić,
Dino Delibašić)
2021–

125 B

Sarajevo, surrounded by mountains with awe-inspiring vistas, surprisingly lacks man-made viewpoints. However, a contemporary and sleek new addition is being constructed on the site of the old Trebević Viewpoint. Significantly larger than its wooden predecessor, it responds to the increased need for a refuge in nature. The viewpoint is in proximity to the cable car landing and connected with a road to the Bobsleigh & Luge Track and the Hotel Pino (Prvi Šumar). Drawing inspiration from the geometry of the surrounding mountains, the building has a triangular shape extending outward from the hillside directing views towards Sarajevo. Its form is deconstructed into two intersecting elements, which adds to the dynamic expression and with a slanting ramp relates to the surrounding terrain. By blending into the surrounding landscape and reflecting the sky and nature, this high-tech material creates a relationship with it. Functionally, it is divided into three horizontal segments. A sunken floor hosts office spaces and conference halls, while the ground floor features a restaurant and bar with a terrace opening towards the city. Using the ramp along the south-east façade, one reaches the rooftop deck that provides a spectacular panoramic view.

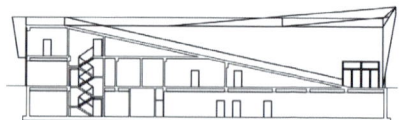

Studio Arh

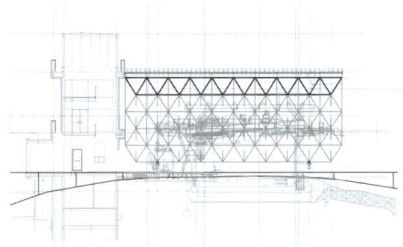

former Yugoslavia and one of the rare ones that functioned from the centre of a city. It was also one of the first objects to be occupied and demolished at the start of the war in 1992. The new stations were placed in the same positions as the initial ones, sharing a similar concept and materiality – stone, glass, high pressure laminate panels, and polycarbonate sheets. The structure is held up by reinforced concrete and brick, but the greater span of the deck is achieved with a space truss anchored to the main structure of the building. This is the most outstanding feature of both the lower and the upper stations of the cable car. The Mero type lightweight construction, as steel tubes tied together with spherical nodes, are covered with polycarbonate sheets in an opal colour. This is the area where visitors can access the gondolas and ride the cable car for its total length of 2,157 m.

Trebević Cable Car Stations

126 D

Hrvatin, Mt. Trebević
IPSA institute, Mufid Garibija,
Adi Muminović, Mirza Bašalić
2018

The cable car has been a connecting line between Sarajevo and the mountain of Trebević since 1959 when it was originally constructed by František Šup, a Czechoslovakian engineer. It was one of the most important cable cars of the

3

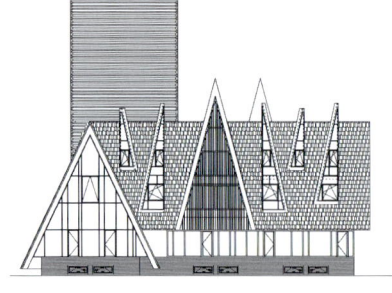

Damir Dautbegović

Damir Dautbegović

Hotel Pino

Ravne 1, Mt. Trebević
Studio ZEC
2014–2015

127 B

3

Hotel Pino is positioned on the slopes of Mt. Trebević at 1,070 m above sea level, ten minutes' drive from the city centre and ten minutes' walk from the Trebević cable car's exit station. It was constructed on the ruins of Sarajevo's popular Prvi Šumar picnic area. The ground and underground horizontal portions of the building are the first where the intense circulation of guests happens. Large terraces on the building's south and west sides are frequently occupied by individuals seeking a quick escape from the city centre and a chance to breathe some fresh air. A neutral, cube-shaped tower with wooden planks on the north-east side holds exclusively hotel rooms. The distinctive identity of this hotel is created by the roof volume, which is highly fragmented with distinctive spiky endings through which the hotel rooms receive light. The architect was inspired by the local vernacular architectural language in the mountains, which relies on adaptation to climate and spatial setting, referencing unique spiky elements on the roof as an interpretation of rural house roofs and the silhouettes of pine trees. All roofs are clad with traditional mountain wood shingles, but the core load-bearing structure is reinforced concrete for practical and economic reasons. The dualism of these two materials is emphasised through the interior – the relationship between warm wooden surfaces and rough concrete. The large open interior space of the ground is divided into a number of smaller isolated zones that are scenographically connected but warm and intimate.

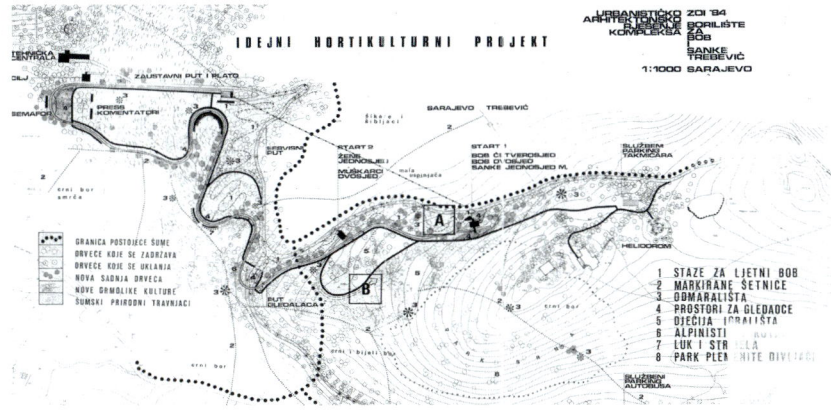

IDEJNI HORTIKULTURNI PROJEKT

1 STAZE ZA LJETNI BOB
2 MARKIRANE ŠETNICE
3 ODMARALIŠTA
4 PROSTORI ZA GLEDAOCE
5 DJEČIJA IGRALIŠTA
6 ALPINISTI
7 LUK I STRELA
8 PARK PLEMENITE DIVLJAČI

The Bobsleigh & Luge Track
Apelova cesta, Mt. Trebević
Gorazd Bučar, Živojin Vekić,
Nebojša Krošnjar
1982

 128 B

Nested in the forests of Mt. Trebević are the remains of the Bobsleigh & Luge Track built during preparations for the 1984 Winter Olympics. Several clever aspects contributed to the project becoming one of the most advanced tracks in terms of construction and technology – even nowadays. The combined bob and luge track, modelled on the 1976 Innsbruck Olympic track, will later become a standard in the winter sports world. The chosen site for the track on the north side of Trebević minimised the need for both cooling and shading. Costs were further reduced through the use of the shotcrete method, in which the bed is laid by spraying the concrete onto the reinforced steel substructure. This was the first instance of such a process being used on a bob and luge track. It is 1,570 m long, or 1,900 m if you consider the two recreational exit-stop ramps. Straight sections are accompanied by 13 curves with an average longitudinal slope of 10.2 per cent and a maximum of 15 per cent, making it one of the steepest and fastest tracks in the world. It was made in three sections that can be separated or combined into tracks for racing, training, or recreation, expanding its use to year-round. Pedestrian trails along the majority of the track allowed spectators to become part of the experience. The track was on the frontline during the Siege of Sarajevo and suffered heavy damage. In the aftermath, the area was dotted with landmines and inaccessible for almost two decades. Alternate uses started to emerge in this context. In the beginning, the track was a popular graffiti canvas, and later as a place for walking, running, and extreme sports. This way, the structure was gradually reintroduced to everyday life of Sarajevo, becoming an informal symbol of rebellious resilience.

3

Irhana Šehović

Anida Krečo

Greenpark Symphony Office Building

129 B

Zlatna Dolina 1, Mt. Trebević
Studio Nonstop (Sanja Galić-Grozdanić, Igor Grozdanić)
2017–2020

Greenpark Symphony is a modern IT park located on the outskirts of Sarajevo in the lower zone of Mt. Trebević at an elevation of 800 metres above sea level. While providing a high-tech working environment in a natural setting, it also opens up the mountain by offering a variety of outdoor recreational activities. It is only ten minutes by car from the city centre and getting there from the city centre requires a half-hour uphill walk through semi-urban neighbourhoods. The site is defined by hilly terrain to the north and west, with open views to newer parts of Sarajevo on one side and a dense forest background on the other. As the first technology centre in Bosnia and Herzegovina, it follows the global trend of modern office spaces with high-tech features. It also accommodates conference rooms and lounges, terraces with views of the whole city, promenades for walking meetings, and a cinema hall for presentations. The centre strives to become a new symbol of contemporary Sarajevo and Trebević, encouraging younger generations to work and have fun in a completely different context away from the polluted urban zones. Long ramps and repeated terraces serve to distinguish the volume's various cascading segments, which follow the steep terrain. This configuration makes the building more inviting to visitors and strives to

Anida Krečo

Sumeja Čakalović

blend into the natural setting while concealing a significant amount of built space. The gentle interior ramps follow the same pattern all the way up to the top of the building. The resulting cross section allows for overlapping views downwards toward the city through interior spaces and external ramps, thus creating a unique experience of being between the city and nature.

Roof Gardens
Mixed-use Building

130 B

Zlatna Dolina nn, Mt. Trebević
Studio Nonstop (Sanja Galić-Grozdanić, Igor Grozdanić) + Filter (Nedim Mutevelić, Vedad Islambegović, Asmir Mutevelić, Kenan Vatrenjak, Ibrica Jašarević)
2019–2023

3

As a continuation of the Greenpark IT Complex, at an even greater altitude of 880 metres above sea level, this mixed-use building sits on a plateau with incredible views stretching from Sarajevo's Old Town and centre to newer parts of the west towards Igman and Bjelašnica mountains. This opportunity for various panoramic views led to the configuration of an elongated strip that goes up and down in section, following the octagonal shape in its layout. This makes the central public square and the negative spaces under the building create a frame for the view of the city and mountains. On the back side, an extended amphitheatre opens up to the forest, creating a place for future city events. The building's formal appearance is reminiscent of the historic fortifications seen on Sarajevo's hills, while the building itself gives the sensation of being close to the city but isolated in nature.

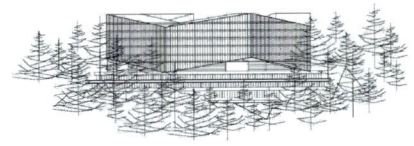

Anida Krečo

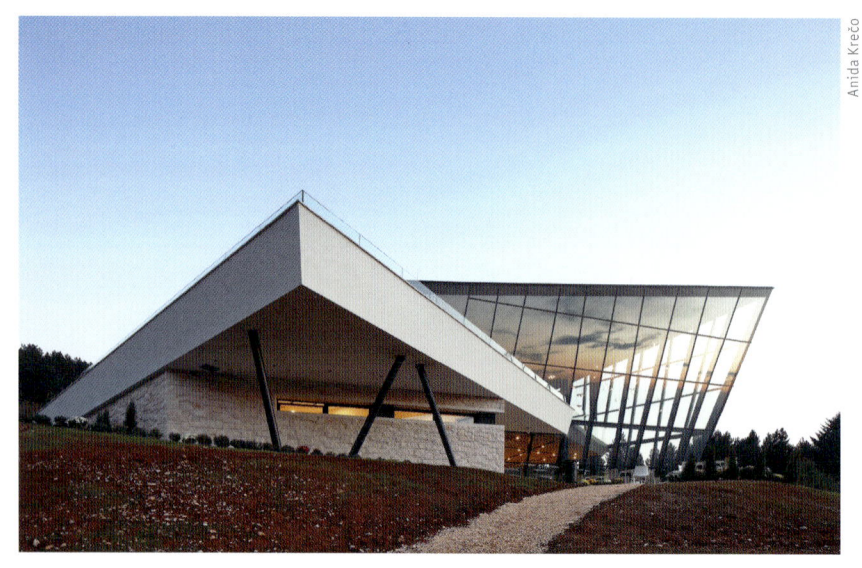

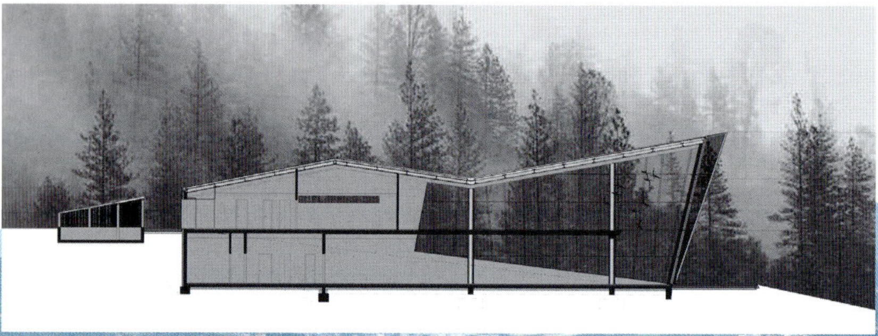

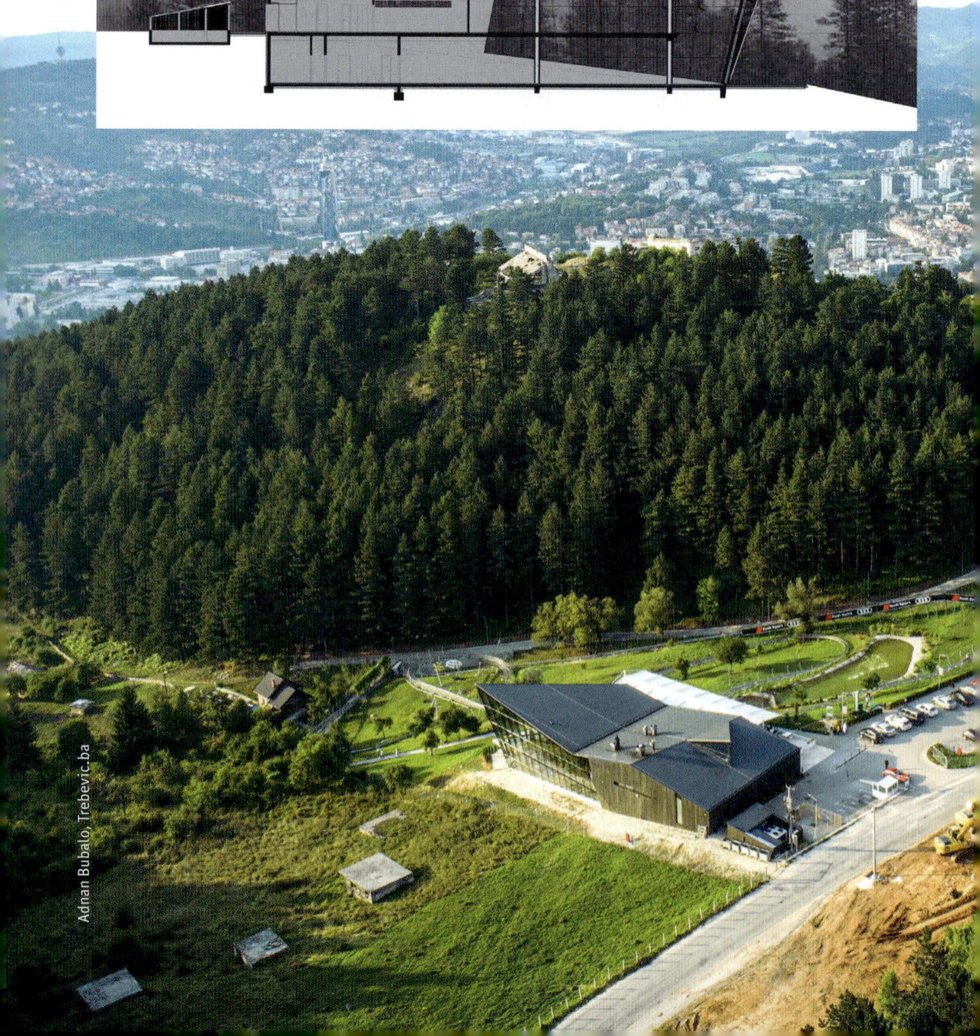

Adnan Bubalo, Trebević.ba

Sunnyland Amusement Park   131 B

Miljevići nn, Mt. Trebević
Kenan Hadžović
2017

Sunnyland Amusement Park is located at an altitude of 800 metres on the edge of Mt. Trebević, a ten-minute drive from Sarajevo city centre. The park's main attraction is the alpine roller coaster, which has a starting station and a track length of 850 metres as well as its auxiliary facilities. The restaurant building is the largest in the park complex and among the facilities of this programme in the Trebević area. The elongated bent roof, which combines the gable and butterfly roofs, gives it its distinctive form.

From the access roadside, the lower scale and mostly enclosed façade clad in dark wooden vertical slats make it more neutral in the natural environment. The roof rises on the north side, offering panoramic views of Sarajevo's newer neighbourhoods, and the geometry becomes more expressive, with a glass façade bevelled in two directions. This design gesture, along with the terrain drop, results in a section of double-height spaces and a completely different appearance towards the city. The crystal-like form of the main transparent volume and the lower solid white cantilever that repeats the similar geometry create a playful visual attraction that corresponds with the amusement park aesthetics.

3

Vraca Memorial

Vraca neighbourhood
Vladimir Dobrović, Alija Kučukalić,
Aleksandar Maltarić
1981

Vraca is a *spomenik* ('memorial') and public space in the heart of Sarajevo, carrying overlapping layers of 130 years of collective memory. The term *spomenik* refers to a series of memorials built in Yugoslavia from the 1950s to the 1990s commemorating resistance against Axis occupation and oppression during the Second World War and embodying the idealism of the national unity that characterised the ex-state. Modernist and abstract, notable in their sculptural quality and materiality, there are tens of thousands of *spomeniks* across ex-Yugoslavia. Covering an area of over 78,000 m², the Vraca *spomenik* is both a Yugoslav era memorial park and an Austro-Hungarian fortress. Its geographical position pre-determined the role the area had in different periods: a fortification on the south end of the city during the Austro-Hungarian period, an execution site for Sarajevans during the Second World War, a citizen resistance and commemoration park in the Yugoslav era, a strategic point for the Serb army in the 1990s, and a neglected area since then. In 1965, the Sarajevo war hero and partisan Vladimir Dugonjić initiated the process to build a memorial in Vraca. However, the international architectural competition did not happen until the end of the 1970s. Vladimir Dobrović's work, previously awarded second prize, was selected to be the new memorial. The works of Sarajevo sculptor Alija Kučukalić were added to Vladimir's architecture, while the landscape concept was developed by Croatian architect Aleksandar Maltarić. The complex officially opened on 25 November 1981. It encompasses several elements with an evident hierarchy in the concept and spatial unit composition. Starting from the main entrance at the south side and its gathering space, towards the west in order are: the eternal flame, the fountain, and a memorial wall symbolising the base of the whole monument with the staircase leading to the Tomb of National Heroes. The tomb is

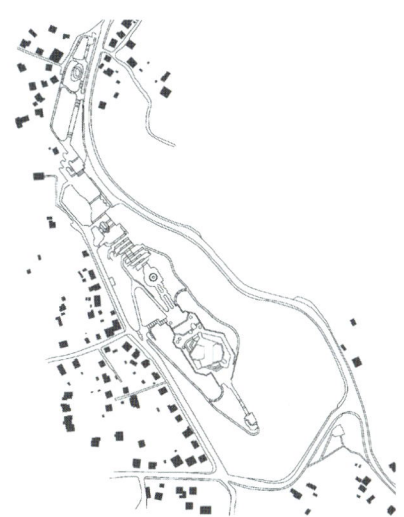

Foto: Irhana Šehović

3

elevated in relation to the entrance, defining its importance in the composition. The top of the hill contains the fortress as well as a 5-metre-tall monument with a relief portraying Josip Broz Tito and a part of his speech from 6 April 1945. East of the main entrance, at the top of the hill is a bronze sculpture depicting a woman with raised arms looking towards the sky; it is a monument to the female soldiers and partisans of the Liberation War. Its very positioning suggests the symbolism of ancient Greek temples. Although declared a national monument, the site has been neglected and in decay for decades, receiving minimal attention. Vraca carries invaluable Sarajevo history in its layers and to this day stands as a symbol of resistance.

Šerafudin's White Mosque by architect Zlatko Ugljen (1979)

Wider Sarajevo
Go Beyond

Wider Sarajevo encompasses the city's broad metropolitan areas outside its administrative and central urban zones and stretches towards an inseparable element of Sarajevo's identity: its mountains. Alongside high altitudes characterised by severe climate conditions, this chapter also covers projects in nearby towns that gravitate towards the capital, expanding on to the diversity of typologies and projects.

In principle, the Sarajevo metropolitan area can be perceived in three main layers. The first central urban layer with the administrative, political, and economic core is covered in the first three chapters. The second layer is the green non-urbanised spaces, mainly the mountains surrounding urban Sarajevo (Igman, Bjelašnica, Treskavica, Jahorina, Romanija, Ozren) with smaller rural units and recently fast-developing ski resorts. The third layer includes an array of clustered and free-standing towns and villages in the Sarajevo functional region, wrapping everything up into one dynamic regional geographical unit.

The chapter includes diverse hospitality typologies, community and public centres, as well as houses of worship, from the newly built, large-scale forest resort enhancing a playful dialogue with nature through to a complete hotel reconstruction aiming to blend new functions into a natural setting. The chapter includes sites from the 1984 Winter Olympics and its monumental ruins – an extensive ski jumping resort on Igman mountain together with the bare concrete structure of a Yugoslav hotel standing as a simultaneous reminder of the 1980s developing society and the 1990s war destruction.

The chapter points out a booming typology of contemporary mountain apartment buildings and hotels as an outcome of an increasing interest in resort skiing. A distinct typology showcased in this chapter are community-driven, small-scale mosques, as well as the guide's highest-altitude project: the Bivouac, constructed with scarce resources and under challenging mountain conditions. Both projects encouraged and engaged a local community of volunteers.

Leaving the mountains and exploring the third layer, the chapter stretches to nearby towns and includes one of the first residential–commercial settlements in Ilijaš in the valley of the Bosna River, planned by Juraj Neidhardt and partly designed using the principle of the unwritten legality of the *right to view*. Wider Sarajevo ends with Šerafudin's White Mosque by Zlatko Ugljen, for which he received the prestigious Aga Khan international award in 1983. It is part of many encyclopaedias of contemporary architecture, masterfully combining contemporary influences and traditional elements. Most of the sites can be reached by car in under 45 minutes from the city centre. For some sites at higher altitudes, we recommend having a local guide.

4

Hotel Termag

Hotel Termag by Studio ZEC (2012)

Anida Kreco

Tarčin Forest Resort
M Gallery
Vilovac nn, Tarčin
AHAKNAP+SAAHA
(Adnan Harambašić, Kenan Brčkalija)
2017

133 A

Built at the foothills of Bjelašnica Mountain by Bosnian-Norwegian architecture practice AHAKNAP+SAAHA, Tarčin Forest Resort enhances a playful dialogue with nature. In the hilly landscape of central Bosnia, the design uses every possibility to understand its microlocation and respond by articulating the design approaches: a light transparent base, a soft border between interior and exterior, architectural forest mimicry, and sensibilities at the cross section of manmade and what is natural. The building layout incorporates two main elements: a longitudinal volume acting as an anchor point with 55 hotel rooms hovering over a public plaza hosting a foyer and a restaurant and 17 villas dispersed in the landscape. Echoing the verticality of the surrounding forest, the primary building volume is covered in slats creating a natural volume expression and blurring the outside/inside perception. The building's core structure is made of reinforced concrete sheets and columns placed to leave as much open space as possible. The façade plasticity is shaped by responding to the main volume and enveloping the ground floor in structural glass panels, and following above-ground areas, leading onto the terrace in stone louvres. The resort's setting in the landscape enabled upper floors of the hotel to seemingly float over a steep hill and act as a natural extension of the Tarčin forest. The porous façade, intricate material choices, and skilful volume definition create a precedent for contemporary hospitality architecture in Bosnia and Herzegovina.

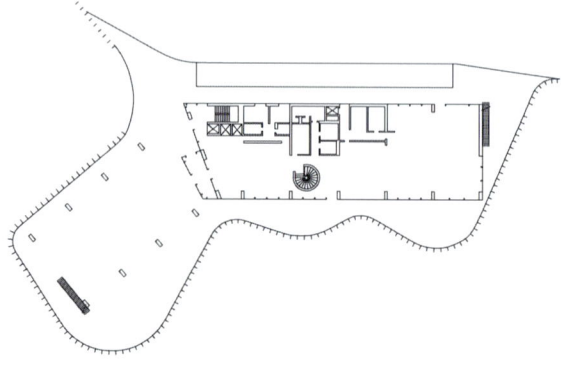

Anida Krečo

NHRV House

134 B

Nahorevo nn
*Filter (Vedad Islambegović,
Ibrica Jašarević, Asmir Mutevelić,
Kenan Vatrenjak, Nedim Mutevelić)*
2012–2014

NHRV House is designed within the socio-economic parameters commonly found in Bosnia and Herzegovina: an underdeveloped construction industry and deregulated urban planning conditions. The composition comprises two sloped volumes – an integrated house and a garage. These volumes adopt a common, generic house shape but are disjointed to align with the fragmented morphology of the surrounding mountain landscape. By arranging the separate volumes together, different sequences of outdoor spaces are formed, harmonising with the house's internal programme. The house's appearance is defined by two materials: a white frame composed

of corrugated metal sheets and wooden infill on the front and back façades. Both materials correspond to the dominant south-north orientation along the slope, capturing sunlight and views. The wooden window blinds, made from the same material as the façade, provide a dual character to the house. When inhabited, they create a scattered, vibrant openness, while when unoccupied, they present a monolithic, restrained appearance.

4

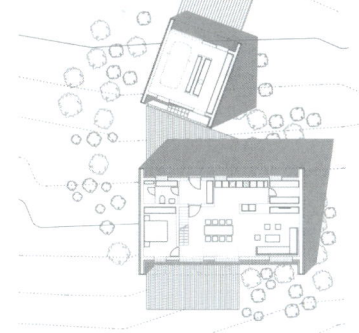

Alter Finjo

Irhana Šehović

Olympic Ski Jumps and Associated Facilities

135 A

Malo polje, Igman Mountain
Janez Gorišek, Vlado Gorišek,
Marko Cotić, Dušan Engelsberger
1982–1984

An autonomous facility for all ski jumping disciplines was built at a height of 1,200 metres above sea level for the 1984 Winter Olympics. A natural amphitheatre with a radius of about 1 kilometre was chosen as the optimal location for the planned facility. The technological scheme of the competitors' movement was the main direction in the design and positioning of all of the structures. Aside from the dominant structures of the ski jumps and the largest building of the ski centre, the entire complex was made up of auxiliary buildings of the bivouac with a buffet and sanitary facilities as well as a tower representing the airstrip. The architecture of the judge's tower located next to the ski jump stands out as a dark monovolume with a steep single-gable roof that follows the slope. Combining Yugoslavia's aspirations for high-quality Olympic infrastructure and an innovative design approach, the ski jumps went on to become standard for future designs. Although it was originally planned to convert the ski centre into a hotel after the Olympics, war destruction in the 1990s made most of the infrastructure useless, though the ski jumps and judge's tower still attract attention.

Hotel Igman
Igman Mountain
Ahmed Džuvić
1983

Designed by Ahmed Džuvić for the XVI Winter Olympic Games, this 164-room hotel is located in close proximity to the grounds for the Nordic disciplines, marathon and biathlon, at the edge of Mt. Igman at 1,226 m above sea level. It is often referred to as one of the most successful hotels of its time in this region for being a constant hub of activity due to its popular location and offer. The challenge with its design was achieving a broad range of functions while respecting the delicate requirements of the mountainous landscape. Although significant in scale, the hotel does not clash with the natural environment, as it is broken down into three hotel wings, limiting the visual comprehension from any single spot. Responding to the genius loci, it seems the architect followed the best practices of Scandinavian architecture in shaping the hotel and in choosing autochthonous materials for the façade cladding. Dramatic sloping and modernist expression provide a dynamic answer to the calm verticals of the spruce forest. Avoiding the repetition and array in its disposition, as well as the orthogonal layout on certain floors, a composition of various angles, heights, and spatial experiences was achieved. The hotel is horizontally divided into three clear segments. The ground floor with shared and public facilities is in exposed concrete. The middle segment with private rooms and slanted walls was clad with natural wood in yellow, while opposite-slanting represented mixed use and was clad in dark Eternit. The hotel was held as a strategic war position in the 1990s. The initial damage was made worse in 1993 when the whole hotel caught fire, and it has remained in a state of decay ever since. In recent years, this representative of Sarajevo modernist heritage has hosted only curious onlookers and hikers exploring the area.

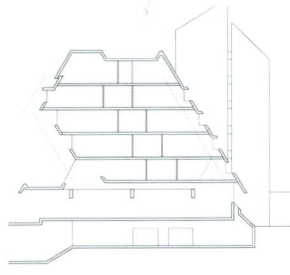

4

Hotel Monti (Feri Hostel)

Mt. Igman, Veliko polje
Kenan Hadžović
2020
Sakib Oković, Dejan Tadić, Zijo Krvavac, (i.d.e..a.) 2003–2004

137 A

Hotel Monti is located in the valley of Veliko Polje (Grand Field) of Mt. Igman on the site of the former devastated building of the BiH Ferial Association Hotel, which served as the starting target house during the XIV Winter Olympic Games. In addition to the need for total reconstruction, the project largely required an increase in square footage because the existing accommodation capacities were neither sufficient in terms of size nor number. Due to the plot's limited size, additions to the building were constructed on both open plot space and on parts of the existing building. The basic idea behind the expansion was to add two blocks on opposite sides of the existing building – east and west – while retaining vertical communication and extending horizontal communication. The extended blocks have five floors: a basement, a ground floor, and three upper floors. There are common public hotel spaces in the basement and ground floor and guest rooms on the upper floors. Despite the fact that this reconstruction significantly increased the building's size, the materials and details preserved the distinction of three pyramidal shearing volumes. As a clear formal allusion to the *katun*, a rural shepherd's hut for nomadic life in the area, this design gesture attempts to minimise the visual impact on the surrounding environment.

Anida Krečo

Bojan Marijanović

Ski Apartments Unioninvest

Babin Do, Mt. Bjelašnica
Studio Nonstop (Sanja Galić-Grozdanić, Igor Grozdanić)
2004–2006

138 A

The Ski Apartments Unioninvest complex was constructed in the Babin Do valley on Bjelašnica Mountain amid a social environment where this popular ski resort is experiencing significant pressure from private apartment investments. The site is characterised by its steep south slope, offering unobstructed views of the ski slopes and the mountain's summit. The primary focus of the building's programme is ski apartments, complemented by retail space and a car park. It consists of four distinct volumes, each comprising 78 apartments with panoramic views of the ski slopes and the mountain peak. According to the architects, the design is influenced by traditional alpine buildings in the region, incorporating elements inspired by the shapes of the mountains. This creates an artificial topography that harmonises with the natural surroundings of mountains, forests, rocks, and snow through the use of a complementary design and materials. After 15 years, this complex continues to stand out as an exemplary demonstration of the balance between large-scale development and sensitivity towards the mountain ambiance.

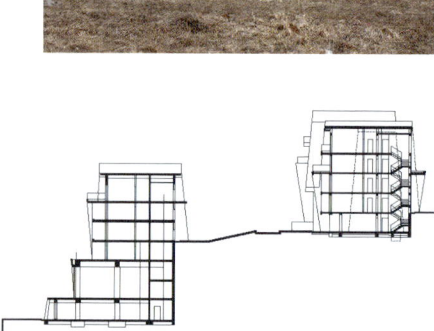

Munever Salihović

Studio Nonstop

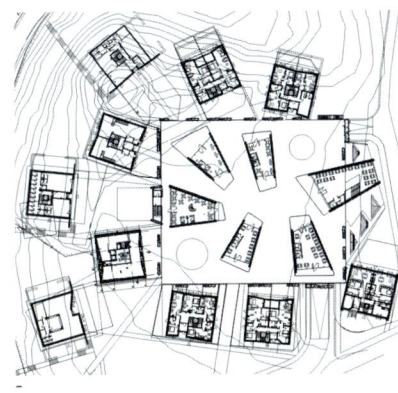

Srebrna Lisica Apartments

Babin Do, Mt. Bjelašnica
Studio Nonstop (Sanja Galić-Grozdanić, Igor Grozdanić)
2014–2019

139 A

4

In 2006, Studio Nonstop developed a project called Hybrid Village at the same site as the Srebrna Lisica Apartment complex. It consisted of a below-grade platform topped by a loose, village-like group of small-scale buildings. A few years later, due to the increasing demand for apartments in the Babin Do valley near the ski lifts, the complex evolved into a cluster of ten identical four-storey buildings spread around the central space above the underground garage. This expansion exceeded the original vision of the Hybrid Village project. However, the goal of creating a village-like atmosphere through the organic dispersion of volumes was still maintained. To enhance this concept, the repetition of volumes and materials was implemented to evoke a sense of visual serenity.

Studio Nonstop

Hotel Han
Babin Do, Mt. Bjelašnica
Studio ZEC
2008–2009

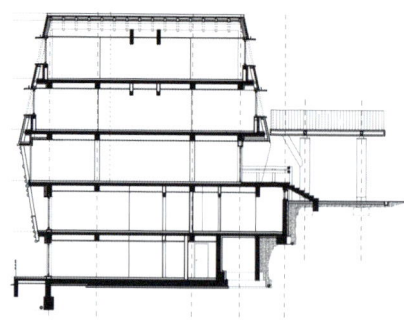

Hotel Han is a renovation of a partially completed building overlooking the Bjelašnica ski slopes. The architect attempted to replicate the building in a winter setting by cladding the entire monovolume in white metal sheets with a symbolic reference to the mountain's name, Bjelašnica ('white mountain'). Given the nature of Mt. Bjelašnica, the design is driven by practical issues and avoids the use of open terraces, leaving openings only where necessary. The white theme is carried throughout the interior, with woollen floor coverings serving as inspiration. The furniture is upholstered for added comfort, creating a relaxing environment. The existing building's height was preserved, but with a more effective section. The ground-floor restaurant is defined by a central navel-like fireplace and divided into several functional units, while the café is designed so that patrons can sit by the window with a view of the ski slopes.

Anida Krečo

Vedad Kasumagić

Panorama Sole Apartments 141 A

Babin Do, Mt. Bjelašnica
Mirsad Hadžirović,
Vedad Kasumagić
2007–2010

This apartment building is located just next to the hotel built before the Winter Olympics, on a south-facing slope. It comprises two parts: a residential component with 22 apartments on four floors and a commercial component with car parks cut into the rocky terrain. This bottom layout distinctively curves around the edge of the terrace leading to the main entrance. The slightly slanted roof plane and sides give the main white cube the appearance of leaning, which is reinforced with the horizontality of wooden shutters covering apartment loggias. Smaller white cubes act as additional accents. Wood, a natural material that conforms to the mountainous environment, is used to highlight the contrast in colour and materialisation while the building's appearance changes due to variations in open and closed shutters.

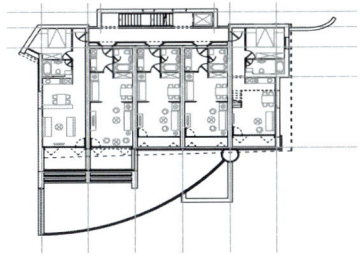

4

Govza 1 Apartments

Babin Do, Mt. Bjelašnica
Nihad Babović / hmd architects
2018

142 A

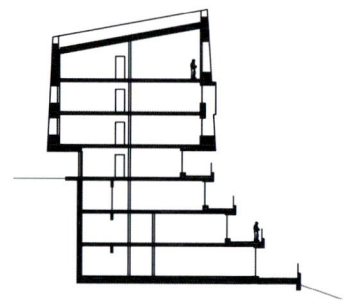

A building is planned for Olympic mountain Bjelašnica's second urban planning phase along and beneath the road, with views of the mountain's peak and ski slopes as well as the potential for direct access to the slopes. The ground and upper three floors with apartments overlook Babin Do and the ski slopes, with three basement floors with apartments, storage rooms, and a shared ski room. The apparent design reference was the *katun*, a rural shepherd's house for nomadic life on Bjelašnica Mountain. The basement levels of the building follow the slope of the terrain towards the ski areas, and its terraces resemble isohypses. Above the ground floor is the *katun*,

a three-storey mountain roof form with three distinctly shaped tin volumes. The playful roof forms, openings, materials, and colours attempt to capture the spontaneity of naive creativity with high-tech detail. While two street entrances with an elevator and a staircase lead to the building, there is an exit with a shared ski room in the centre of the building on the lowest floor, sheltered from the wind and leading to the valley of Olympic Mt. Bjelašnica.

Govza 2 Apartments ←

Babin Do, Mt. Bjelašnica
Nihad Babović / hmd architects
2020

143 A

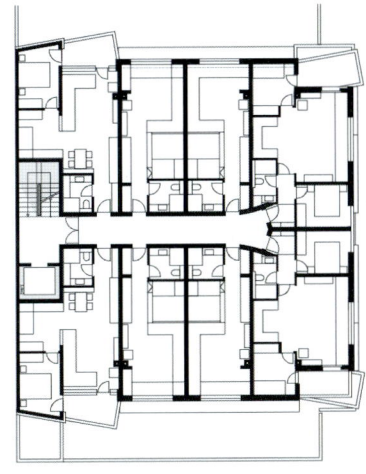

This apartment building is located above the road and the Govza 1 building, and it includes three floors of garages, four floors of apartments, and two two-storey penthouses with terraces. The programmatic discrepancy in size between garages and apartments stems from an intention to share with Govza 1, as car access to the lower floors of Govza 2 was more convenient. Along with this, the extremely steep terrain and the existing massive rock were deciding factors in this project. The entrances are located on two sides of the rock, creating a distinctive appearance of an apartment building jutting over it. The shape and size of the apartment part is set back from both sides of the garage, so every apartment in the building has a view of the top of Bjelašnica, Babin Do, and the ski slope. As with Govza 1, this project aims to pull refences to traditional architecture in a mountainous environment and lower the scale impression by introducing the scattered roof planes. A special feature of the building are balconies in irregular shapes between the sloping roof planes and glass surfaces.

4

Nihad Babović

Edvin Kalić

Hotel Nomad

Babin Do, Bjelašnica
TEAMM, NOX BIRO
(Vedad Kasumagić, Feđa
Hadžibegović, Lamija Salihbašić,
Adnan Makić, Haris Kurtanović,
Tamara Koroman, Nedim Smajević,
Iskra Leko)
2023

144 **A**

As a part of an area experiencing rapid development close to the ski resort of Bjelašnica, Hotel Nomad represents a programmatic advance in contrast to the vast majority of the recently constructed apartment buildings. In addition to the hotel rooms, a spa and wellness centre with a large swimming pool and an additional conference room for business meetings and events are located on an area of about 12,000 square metres. The striking sight of the hotel's eaves, which are supported by a series of V-pillars, welcomes visitors as they approach the main entrance from the south-east. When viewed from the side of the hill, the building appears to be a three-volume structure that floats over the lower, sunken floors. The accent is created by a lower, floating volume with a large panoramic opening from the swimming pool area to the surrounding forest and ski trails. Wrapping balconies of all projecting volumes in repetitive vertical slats provide the voluminous structure with the appearance of flickering and lightness in a natural environment.

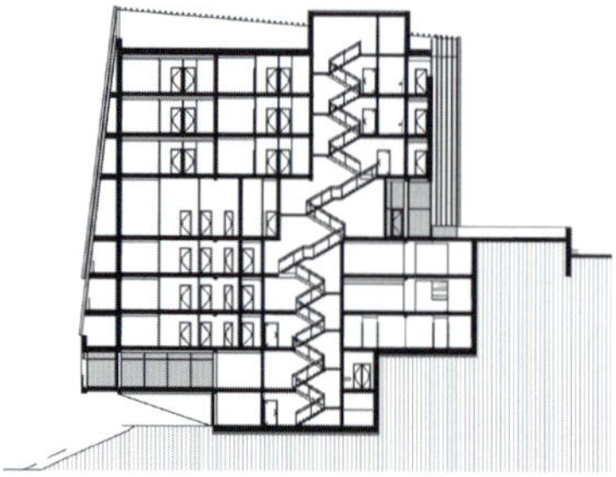

Edvin Kalić; Interior: Mecolada

Apartments Štini do

Štini do, Bjelašnica
NOX BIRO, TEAMM (Vedad Kasumagić, Feđa Hadžibegović, Nedim Smajević, Lamija Salihbašić)
2018

Sarajevo residents are increasingly seeking a getaway from everyday life, city air, and noise pollution. In addition to tourism during the winter months, such a lifestyle concept has popularised going to the mountains for rest and recreation on a daily, weekly, monthly, or annual basis. As a result, the demand for owned flats and rooms for rent in mountain tourist areas has surged in recent years. Two similar buildings are located beneath the steep slopes of Bjelašnica and among the canopy of conifers. Its distinct location stands out due to its proximity to the ski slope while being far enough away from the main centre of winter events in Babin Do. The two buildings adhere to the same approach, adapting to the terrain's configuration, beginning with the base volume of parking garages and growing to the main volume containing apartments. The repeating A-frame outlines generate the unique shape, slightly varying its lowest and highest point from one side of the building to the other, attempting to blend into the surrounding forest.

4

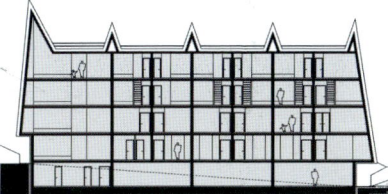

Ivan Bošnjak

Sandro Lendler

Mosque Ostojići

146 A

Ostojići, Mt. Bjelašnica
Studio ZEC
2007

Sandro Lendler

This project demonstrates the transformation of a simple hut into a contemplative space in Ostojići, a village on the slopes of Mt. Bjelašnica. The villagers' desire to build their own-funded mosque with assistance from an architect was the starting point of this project. Understanding the synergy of 'good intentions' of people who are of one mind, the architects exerted great sensitivity in creating a basic idea suitable to the setting, religious principles, and local people's needs. The design was carefully considered in order to construct a mosque that would truly be the people's own, built with their own hands. The architects perceive the village mosque as part of a whole – 'the vortex of the village to which everything comes and from which everything goes'. With the inviting porch at the front of the building, the ground plan is oval, recalling the form of a Muslim's hands held in prayer, which is also a shape that 'brings together' the local people. The form relies on a typical hut with a common roof in this area, with just the vertical wooden

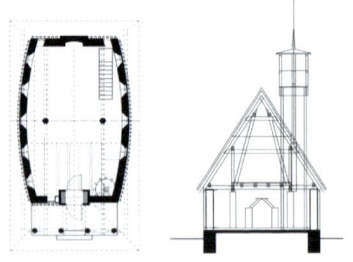

minaret distinguishing it as a house of worship. The building's elliptical body is coated with wooden posts that disguise the openings, and the roof is clad with shingles while the interior design was thought out and completed entirely by local residents.

Bivouac 'Zoran Šimić'

Mt. Visočica
*Filter (Kenan Vatrenjak,
Nedim Mutevelić,
Asmir Mutevelić, Ibrica
Jašarević, Vedad Islambegović)*
2019

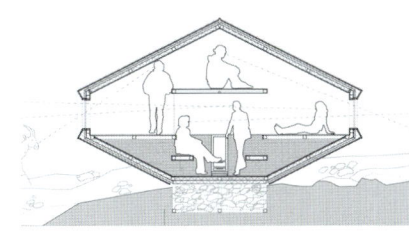

This bivouac is hidden away on the isolated mountain of Visočica near the edge of the Rakitnica canyon, which separates it from the adjacent Bjelašnica Mountain. It is one of the rare places where walking pathways bridge the canyon and link the two mountains. Because of recent improvements to the local road network, it is the first build of this typology on the mountain. Beautiful panoramas unfold at the location, mostly along the north-south axis. The project is designed to expose the visitor to these sights, keep them at the forefront of their minds, and enhance the experience. Interior space is divided into three platforms that serve as floor spaces, beds, or seats. Up to nine people may sit opposite each other on two opposed platforms that cascade towards the entryway. The interior platform layout is followed by the exterior shape to reduce the structure's footprint and reduce destructive excavations. The structure is tightly covered in metal sheets to protect against the severe winds that are

Emir Handžić

typical of this region, and tensioners are also used to anchor the construction at four points. The bivouac was constructed with very few resources, in challenging high mountain conditions, and with a huge amount of volunteer participation and collaboration, which is something that would be unimaginable in a commercial project scenario. It is an example of a sincere, community-driven project that has received significant media attention and continues to draw tourists to enjoy the breathtaking natural beauty of this region.

4

Jadran Ćilić

Hotel Termag

Olimpijska, Mt. Jahorina
Studio ZEC
2012

Hotel Termag is located at an altitude of 1,550 m at the Jahorina Olympic Centre's entry plateau, Poljice, and next to the slopes and ski lifts. The project is an extension of the main hotel building constructed in 2005. Its original size was more than doubled by adding four floors of living space, meeting rooms, and wellness facilities on the ground floor. Walls with a sloped roof that rise from one storey next to the existing structure to four floors on the other side define the upper volume. All visible roof panels are covered with wooden shingles. The loggias on the two major façades of apartments are covered with natural-finish timber verticals that intimate the spaces by interpreting the traditional *mushebak* screen wall. Furthermore, the hotel's whole interior and furniture are made of solid wood. The fact that the hotel's owner runs a sawmill and engages in carpentry explains the extensive use of wood, which contributes to the hotel's warm appeal within the snowy landscape.

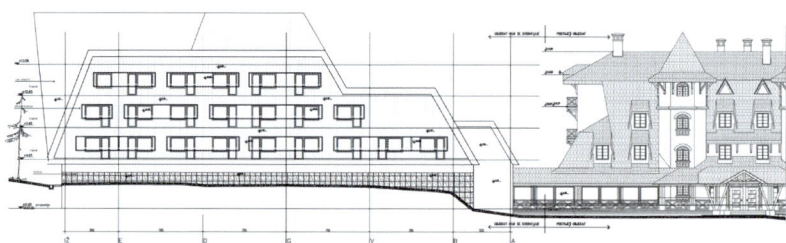

Studio SWITCH

Anida Krečo

4

Olimpijska kuća
149 A

Olimpijska, Mt. Jahorina
Lejla Hasibović (Butmir)
2018–2019

Olimpijska kuća (Olympic House), named after the street, is an addition to a previously existing commercial building. On a slight incline running from south to north, it is situated directly across from the Jahorina Olympic Centre's entrance plateau, Poljice. It is divided into two distinct programmatic and formal parts: the lower section has four garage bays that can fit up to five cars, several commercial spaces, and a personal restroom; and the upper eight levels are composed of apartments. Large window openings that provide impressive views of Mt. Jahorina's ski slopes function as a distinctive feature of the apartments. The small lot size and the densely populated ski resort environment appear to have contributed to the building's proportion. Its contemporary design – a bent monovolume with a sharp end – intends to make it less obtrusive but unique among other buildings.

Half-A-Frame Cabin
150 A

Vučja Luka, Mt. Crni Vrh
Nedim Mutevelić, Asmir Mutevelić,
Jonus Ademović
2022

The cabin is placed 1,300 m above sea level on steep and densely forested terrain with beautiful views of the mountains and valley. The harsh continental climate, with heavy winter snowfall, favours the A-frame as a typical and traditional weekend house typology in the area. To address the site restrictions, such as the steepness of the terrain, as well as its benefits, such as the opportunity for spectacular views, a radical reinterpretation of the A-frame typology was created. As a half-A-frame typology, it enabled various configurations of openings as well as a symmetrical floor plan with a full-height central space facing the deck.

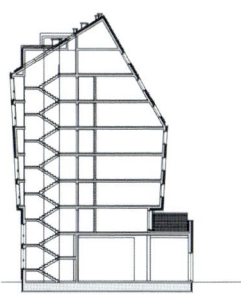

Ilijaš.net

Ilijaš Residential-Commercial Settlement

151 A

Ilijaš town
Juraj Neidhardt
1939–1940

The construction of this residential-commercial settlement in Ilijaš began in 1940. The settlement is in the valley of the Bosna River in the immediate vicinity of the railway and the main road. An iron factory was built opposite the settlement in the industrial zone, with construction continuing after the Second World War. The Ilijaš residential-commercial settlement is one of the first modern settlements built in BiH after 1945. In the settlement, one collective road was planned, from which

residential roads with turnstiles were connected. Part of the settlement, located on the slope, was designed on the principle of the unwritten legality to the 'right to view'. The entire structure was not executed according to Neidhardt's project. A special characteristic of the settlement is the large green areas between the buildings and characteristic residential buildings with four and six apartments under one roof, placed alternately in order to get the best possible views and a larger open area. A recreational zone was designed next to the settlement. During 2013–2014, the reconstruction of the central street was carried out and it was turned into a pedestrian zone. The total length of the street is 300 metres.

4

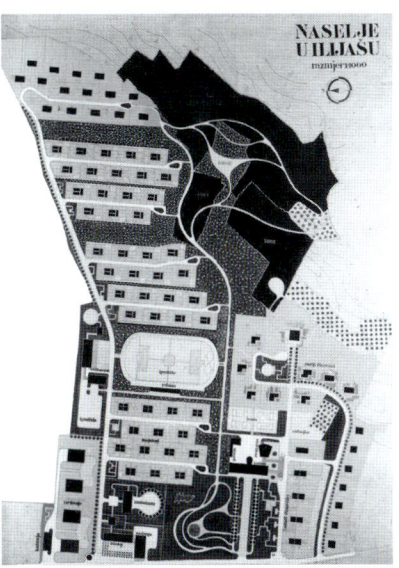

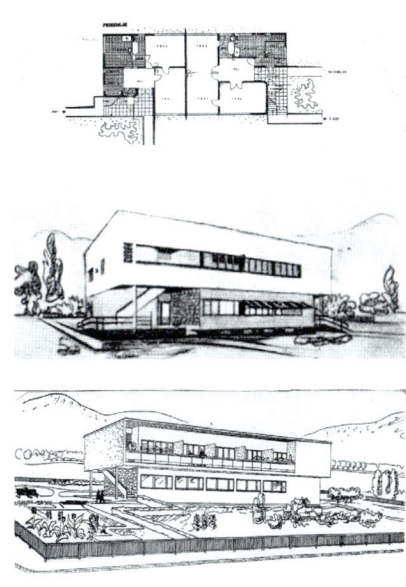

Neidhardt Archive

Masjid Smailbegovići
Smailbegovići, Breza town
Studio MRAV
(Ilma Kobilica, Zejd Kobilica)
2020

Anida Krečo

The masjid is situated within a typical Bosnian suburb, which usually have their own mosque or masjid. In this particular project, the local community took full responsibility for funding and completion, actively encouraging architects to contribute their expertise. It partially occupies private land and is encircled by a steel fence – a sort of veil on the road that separates private spaces from the public. The square floorplan is complemented by a butterfly roof constructed with timber. This design seamlessly blends traditional Bosnian architectural roofing materials with contemporary elements. The windows showcase decorative geometric openings, skilfully concealing those inside while allowing gentle streams of light to permeate the worship area. The inspiration for these geometric patterns stems from the rich tradition of Islamic art ornamentation. Inside, the interior exudes a serene ambiance through the careful implementation of low lighting, an interplay of shadows and light creating an atmosphere of harmony and tranquillity.

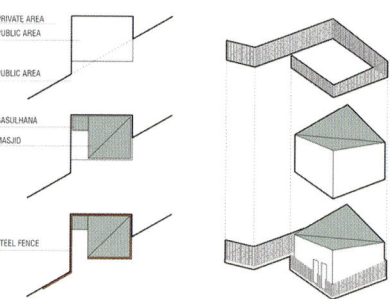

Anida Krečo

Anida Krečo

City Hall Kakanj

153 A

Ulica Branilaca, Kakanj town
Entasis, Vedina Babahmetović
2013

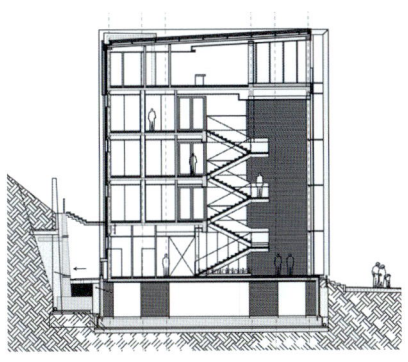

The City Hall Kakanj is strategically positioned adjacent to the exit road from the town of Kakanj and alongside the picturesque Zgošća River, bestowing it with added significance. What makes this structure intriguing is its distinction as one of the relatively newer establishments purposely designed to cater to the specific requirements of municipal administration, with particular emphasis on creating well-organised open spaces for users. Architecturally, the building revolves around a central open hall, flanked by two wings that clearly delineate the administrative floors housing various departments of the municipality on the right and left sides, respectively. Notably, the ground floor accommodates various public amenities such as the counter hall, wedding hall, and council hall. Comprising multiple volumes, the building showcases diverse materialisation and incorporates a rhythmic arrangement of openings, while its distinctive appearance is further defined by the vertical sunshades affixed to its office façades. Spanning an area of 5,500 m², it is one of the rare examples of newly built contemporary municipal architecture buildings in the region around Sarajevo.

Anida Krečo

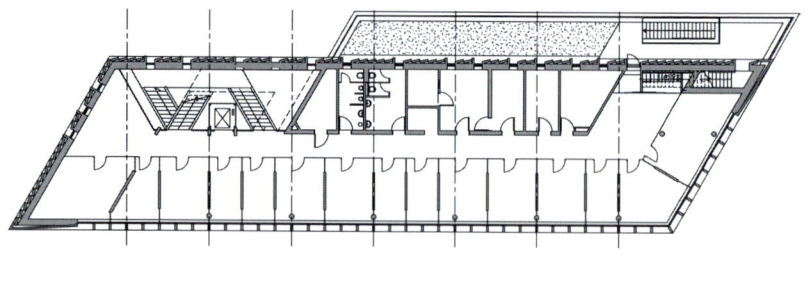

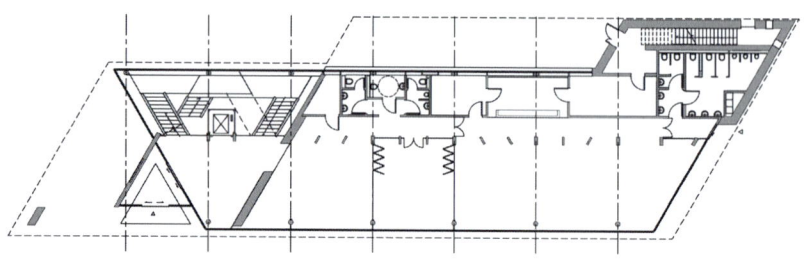

Kakanj Cement Office 154 A

Selima efendije Merda-
novića 146,
Kakanj Kakanj town
Studio Nonstop
(Sanja Galić-Grozdanić, Igor Grozdanić)
2016–2017

The Kakanj Cement Office building designed by Studio Nonstop embodies the use
of exposed concrete, reflecting the client's
core activities in cement and concrete production. Facing south towards the park and
factory, with parking and freight access on

Anida Krečo

the north side, the building features a main entrance in the south-west and a worker's restaurant entrance oriented towards the east. It comprises a basement with archives and storage, a ground floor with an entrance hall, a showroom, a meeting room, and a restaurant, a first floor with administrative offices, and a second floor with management offices and meeting rooms. The ground floor spaces create a versatile area for gatherings and events. The folded free-standing stairs made of precast concrete visually echo the façade elements. Formally, the building represents a volume that incorporates the client's defined design programme and adapts to the former workers' barracks footprint within the Kakanj Cement Factory site. By embracing the local natural materials and responding to the industrial context, the building achieves high social, economic, and ecological standards. It utilises cement and concrete produced from local thermal power plant waste and uses waste energy from the same plant for heating, achieving a significant degree of waste energy and material recycling and promoting environmental sustainability.

4

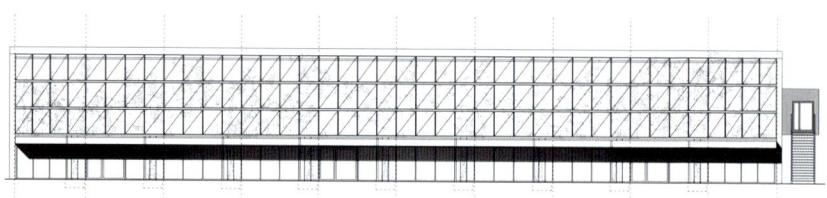

Multifunctional Sports Hall at the Franciscan Gymnasium

155 A

Bosne Srebrene 4, Visoko town
OSNAP – Open South North Architecture Practice (Christoph Hinterreiter, Gorica Mehić, Arijana Šuvak, Anida Krečo)
2019

Construction of the multifunctional sports hall is the first step in the overall redevelopment of the Franciscan complex in Visoko. Founded in 1900, the complex consists of a monastery, a gymnasium, agricultural and sports grounds, and a historic park. The sports hall was placed at the far north-eastern end of the site to create an attractive ending and to move the historic park to the centre of daily life in the complex. A large but very economic envelope was constructed to house the sports field with tribunes, spaces for movement, and service rooms. Two horizontal openings provide natural light and visual links with the historic park. The tribune connects the park level and indoor sportsground. The glazing at park level can be partially opened for large events to enable free circulation between inside and outside. Service rooms are placed in free-standing towers. There is no back side and users are invited to stroll around and programme the space. The sculptural forms of the towers are used for climbing. The façade towards the park is planted with vegetation and in seasonal dialogue with the park.

Anida Krečo

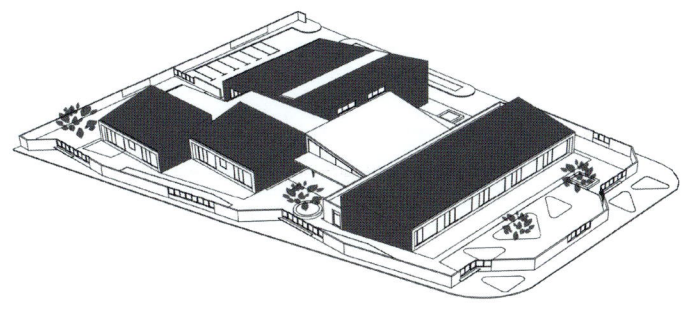

Kindergarten Prijeko

Bosne Srebrene 4, Visoko town
Sinteza arhitektura
(Zijad Sirčo, Jasmin Sirčo)
2014–2023

156 A

The new kindergarten was built on the grounds of the old one, which was almost completely destroyed during the war. It can accommodate 200 children in the nursery and kindergarten age groups. The structure is made up of several segments with single-pitched roofs, each representing a different function within the structure, such as the nursery and kindergarten rooms, a multifunctional hall, the dining room, and so on. Through windows that run almost the entire length of the rooms, an attempt was made to create a connection between the indoor rooms for the children and the terraces that are located outside. Wooden panelling covers the façades of all segments where children frequently move. The programme inside the building is also emphasised by different materialisation, where all communications and social spaces from the outside are in the same materialisation. A multifunctional space with a cascading children's playground was designed in the centre of the building, which is flanked on both sides by large windows. The building's roof structure is made of glued laminated timber beams. An outdoor children's playground is located at the front and side of the building, while the entrance, service area, and car park are located on the rear side. The polygonal fence shields the interior contents and children from the city and its surroundings. The fence enters the interior of the kindergarten complex in some places, creating rest areas and urban furniture on the outside.

4

Šerefudin's White Mosque

157 A

Bijela džamija, Visoko town
Zlatko Ugljen
1969–1979

Šerefudin's White Mosque in Visoko was designed in 1969 in the socialist context of the former Yugoslavia. A modern approach has resulted in a unique solution differing from existing typologies (primarily Ottoman). The design inspiration came from the essence of the Islamic faith and the tale of the Prophet Muhammad's stay in the cave. Ugljen created an artificial concrete cave, quarter compartment-shaped and with five zenithal openings associated with the five daily prayers in Islam. These openings relate to the position of the Sun throughout the day. In 1983, Zlatko Ugljen received the prestigious Aga Khan international award for architecture for his work, and the mosque in Visoko entered almost all encyclopaedias of contemporary architecture. It masterfully combined contemporary influences and traditional Ottoman elements. It is usual for the commission to talk with the architect, investors, contractors, and users of the space in order to gain a better insight into the construction itself and user satisfaction. When the committee for awarding the Aga Khan award arrived,

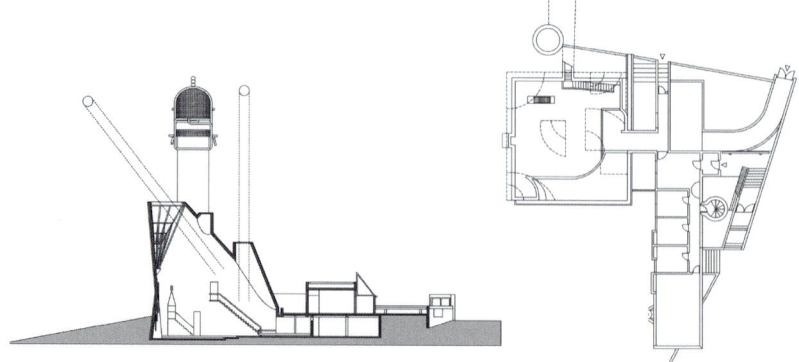

it found an elderly gentleman praying in the mosque area. They asked him for his opinion about the mosque and he told them: 'I personally don't like it, my children will accept it, and my grandchildren will be proud of it.' His comment contributed to the award committee's decision. The relationship with daylight plays a key role in volume creation as well as the atmosphere formation within the projects. Approaches to the use of daylight in spatial design, among them zenithal light, can be traced back through history with the Roman Pantheon as a key predecessor. The author is constantly searching and entering undiscovered areas of architectural expression. The guiding thread in his work is reliance on architectural heritage and its modern transformation and reinterpretation. His projects acquire a universal meaning and language through the use of elements rooted in tradition and a memory of the country where they were created: light-dark relationships, geometric shapes, proportions, and contextualisation.

Monograph *Zlatko Ugljen Architect*

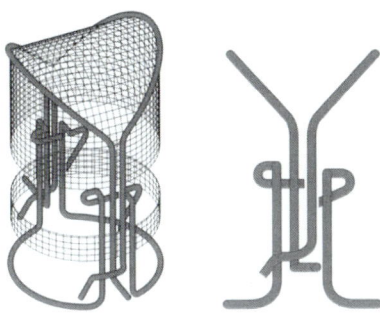

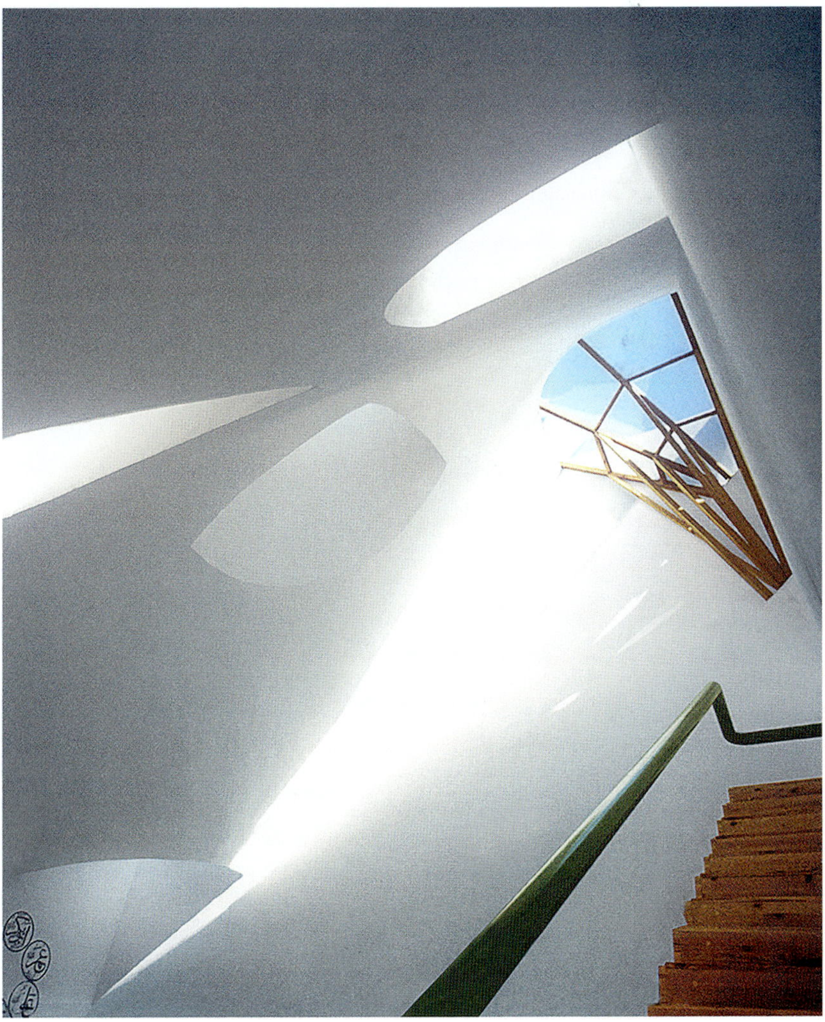

Aerial view of Visoko and Mt. Visočica (2021)

157

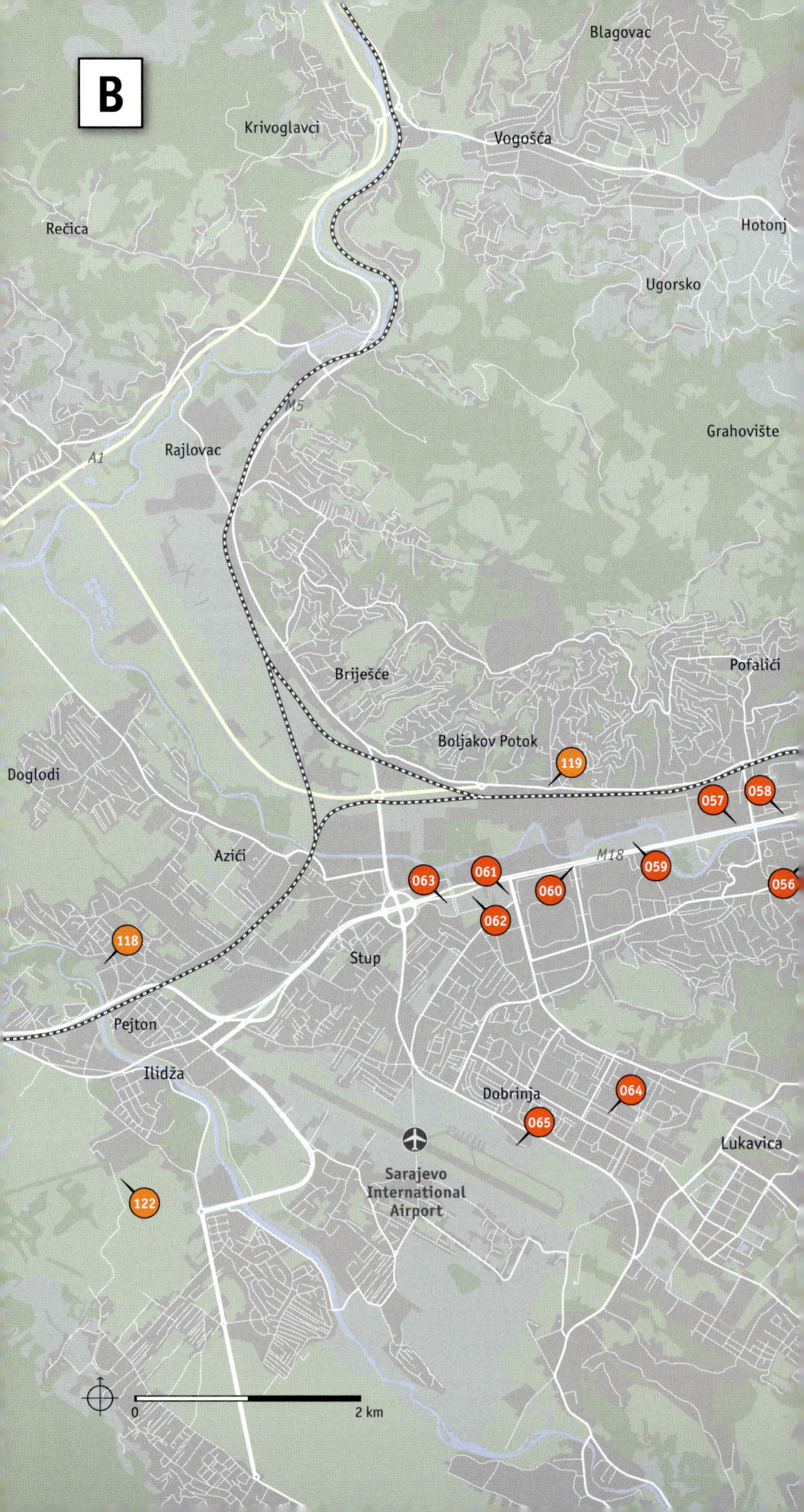

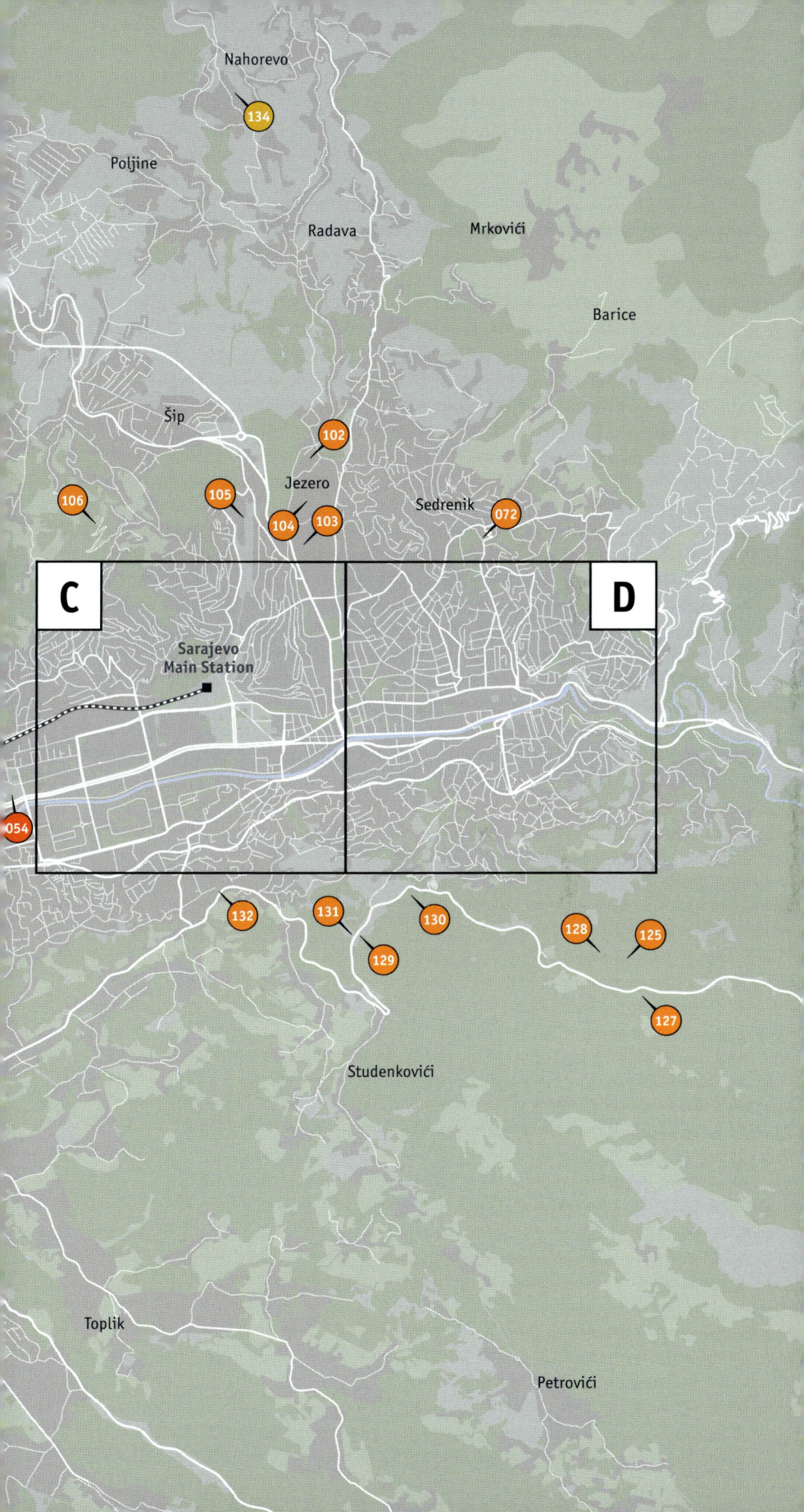

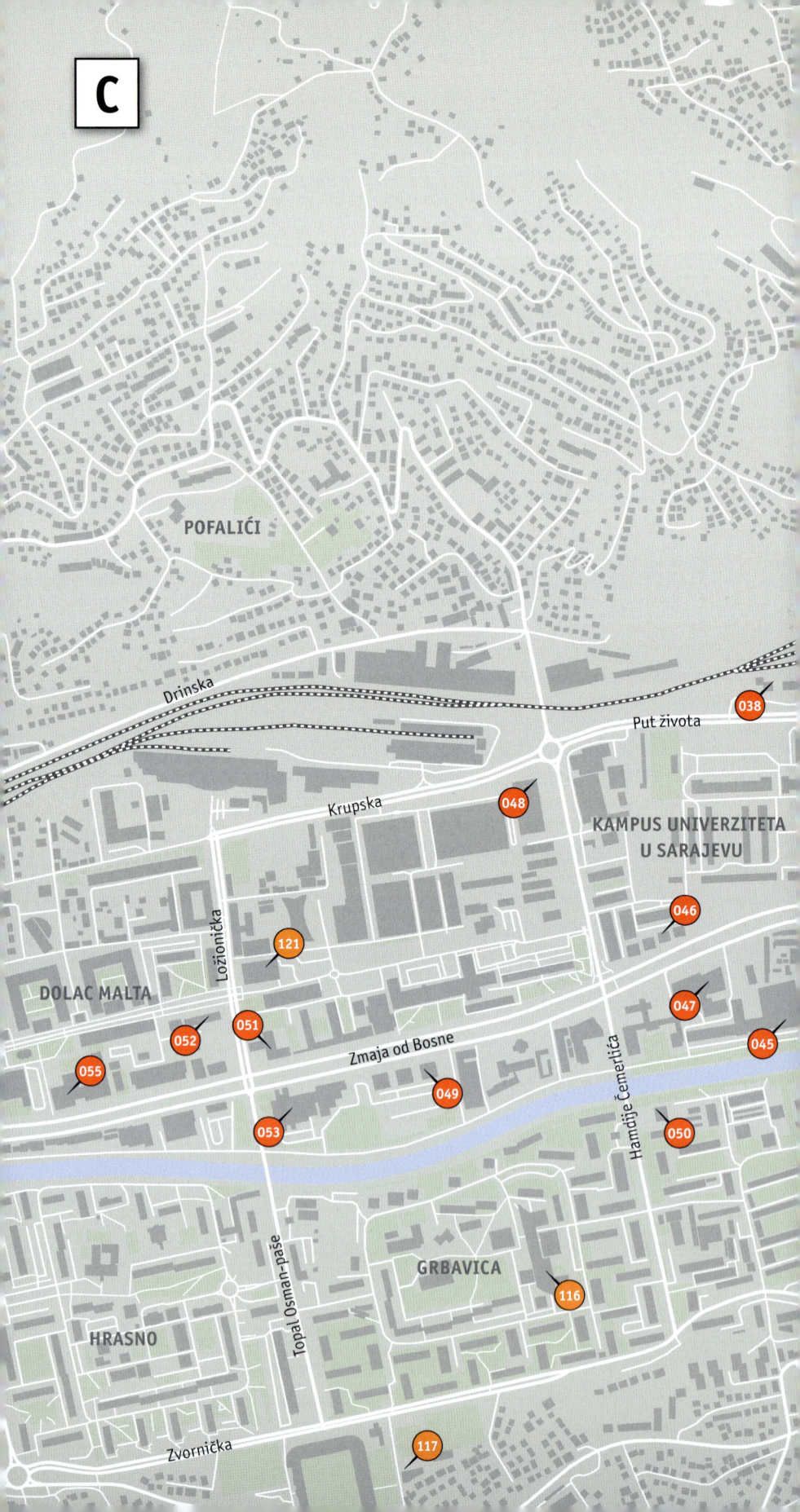

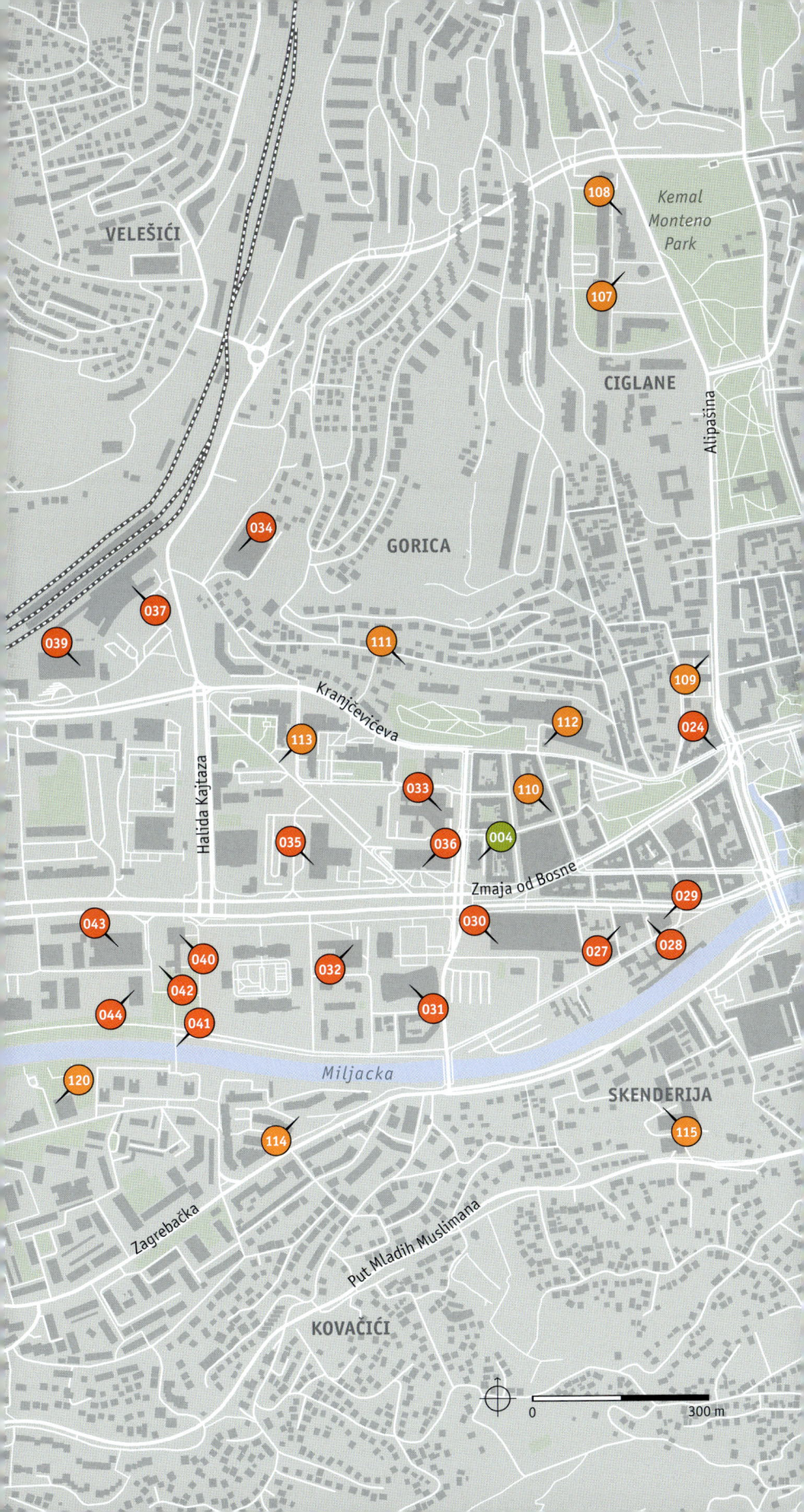

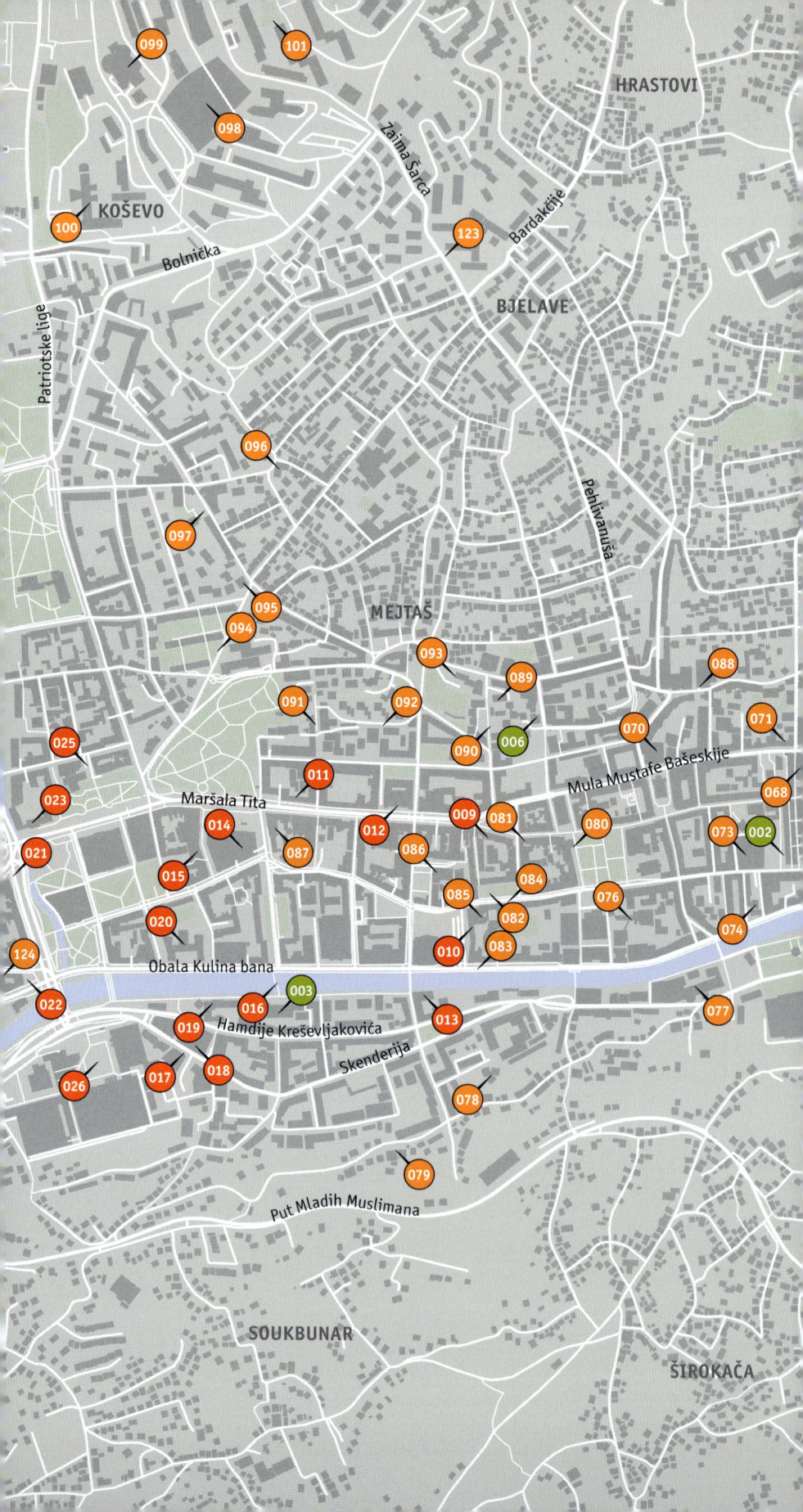

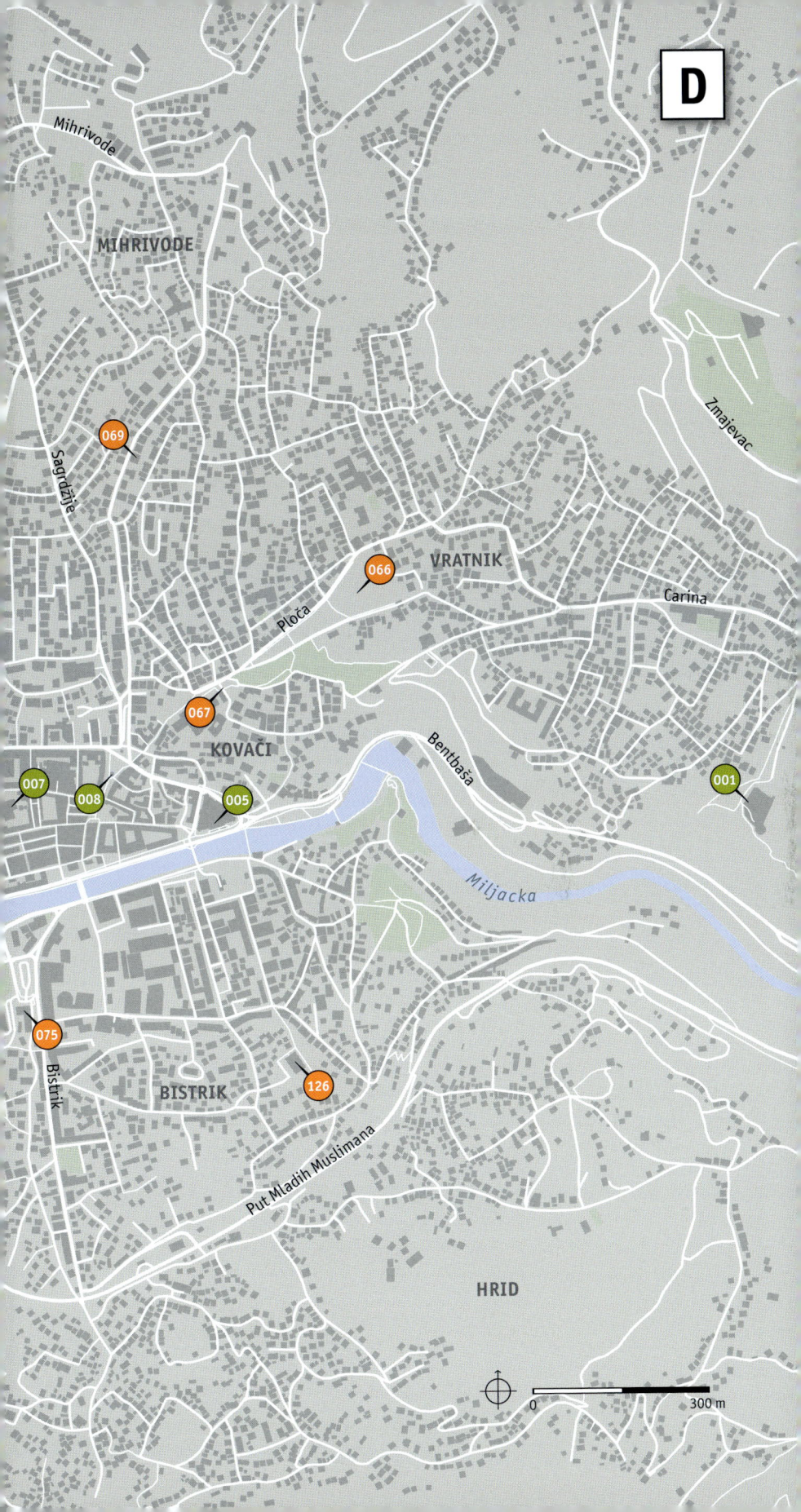

Index of Architects

Sorted by page number

Index of Buildings and Projects

Sorted by project number

Open-air bookshop in Sarajevo's old town

Selected Bibliography

Aganović, Midhat (2009): *Construction and the State of Other Activities in Sarajevo in the 20th and Previous Centuries*. Sarajevo, Štamparija Fojnica.

Aganović, Midhat (2014): *Contemporary Urban, Residential and Communal Dilemmas and Problems of City Development*. Sarajevo, Štamparija Fojnica.

Aganović, Midhat (2009): *Graditeljstvo I stanje drugih djelatnosti u Sarajevu u XX I prethodnim stoljećima*. Sarajevo, IP Svjetlost Sarajevo.

Grabrijan, Dušan, and Neidhardt, Juraj (1957): *Arhitektura Bosne I Hercegovine i put u suvremeno*. Ljubljana, Ljudska pravica.

Husetić, Aida (2019): *Arhitekt / Architect Hasan Ćemalović*. Sarajevo, University press Sarajevo i Magistrat Sarajevo.

Ibelings, Hans (2010): *Restart 1995–2010: arhitektura u Bosni i Hercegovini*. Sarajevo, Buybook.

Kadić, Emir (2010): *Arhitekt Reuf Kadić i početci moderne arhitekture u Bosni i Hercegovini*. Sarajevo.

Kadić Emir (2010): *Architect Reuf Kadić and the Beginnings of Modern Architecture in Bosnia and Herzegovina*. Sarajevo.

Knežević, Snješka (2002): *Arhitekt Ivan Štraus*. Sarajevo, Akademija nauka i umjetnosti Bosne I Hercegovine.

Milošević, Predrag (1997): *Arhitektura u Kraljevini Jugoslaviji*. Sarajevo, Prosvjeta.

Niebyl, D. (2020): *The Architectural Legacy of Sarajevo's '84 Winter Olympics*. <spomenikdatabase.org/post/the-architectural-legacy-of-sarajevo-s-84-winter-olympics>

Redžić, Husref (1983): *Studije o islamskoj arhitektonskoj baštini*. Sarajevo, Veselin Masleša.

Salihović, Erdin (2018): *Svjedočanstvo jednog vremena – Arhitekt Hamdija Salihović*. Sarajevo, Arhitektonski fakultet Univerziteta u Sarajevu.

Stane Bernik (2002): *Architect Zlatko Ugljen*. Tuzla, International Portrait Gallery Tuzla.

Štraus, Ivan (2010): *99 arhitekata sarajevskog kruga 1930–1990*. Sarajevo, Zagreb, Šahinpašić.

Štraus, Ivan (1987): *15 godina bosanskohercegovačke arhitekture*. Sarajevo, IP Svjetlost Sarajevo.

Štraus, Ivan (2013): *Arhitektura Jugoslavije*. Sarajevo, Fondacija za razvoj održivog dizajna.

Trapara, B. (2020): *From Vienna to Sarajevo, Role Models and Replicas in the Architecture of Austro-Hungarian Period*. Sarajevo, International Burch University.

Turato, I. (2014): *Bosanski opus Andrije Čičin Šaina*. <https://www.idisturato.com/blog/2014/11/02/bosanski-opus-andrije-cicin-saina/>

Turkušić Jurić, Elša (2022): *Elementi stambene arhitekture, dnevni boravak kroz vrijeme*. Sarajevo, Arhitektonski fakultet Univerziteta u Sarajevu.

Žuljić, Vlasta-Jelena; Čengić, Nihad H.; Čakarić, Jasenka (2015): *Sarajevo metropola Model razvoja*. Sarajevo, Arhitektonski fakulter Sarajevo AAU Acta Architectonica et Urbanistica Sarajevo.

... and further reading ...

Authors and Contributors

LIFT – Spatial Initiatives is an organisation that was founded by a group of young architects four years after organising the first Days of Architecture Sarajevo festival, aiming to encourage discourse on contemporary architecture, design, and spatial planning, while connecting these topics to global social and cultural changes and focusing on Sarajevo as the main case study. The main activities are focused on the production of architectural / cultural events (lectures, exhibitions, competitions, research / studies and community workshops, spatial interventions, projections etc.) through the international festival Days of Architecture Sarajevo, one of the most recognised architectural events in South-East Europe, held over multiple days annually since 2008. Over ten years, Days of Architecture and LIFT have progressed from a student project to one of the most important events for the contemporary architecture of Bosnia and Herzegovina. The period is marked by a continuous broadening of cooperation with architects, researchers, and professionals from other disciplines and geographies, and a gradual evolution of the approach in designing the festival and the community. Today, DA's focus is on developing a regional platform for networking and complementary education of architects and architecture students. The book *3650 Days of Contemporary Architecture in Sarajevo* (2018, self-published) is a reminder of the collective efforts that, despite extremely unfavourable circumstances in Bosnia and Herzegovina, ensured the continuity and helped build the recognisable character of the festival.

3650 Days of Contemporary Architecture in Sarajevo (2018)

Hubert Klumpner is an architect and co-founder of Urbanthinktank_next. He is considered one of the originators of the social turn, a movement that had its breakthrough in 2010 with the *Small Scale, Big Change: New Architectures of Social Engagement* exhibition at MoMa, New York. He is the Architecture and Urban Design Professor at the Swiss Institute of Technology / Eidgenössische Technische Hochschule Zürich. Urbanthinktank has received numerous awards and prizes such as the Golden Lion of the Venice Architecture Biennale, the Gold Holcim Award Latin America, and the Award for the Best Educational Building from the Chicago Museum of Architecture and Design. Recent built projects include *Fabrica de Cultura* and the *ONDA Green Corridor Project* in Medellin, Colombia.

Michael Walczak is an architect and co-founder of Urbanthinktank_next. He holds a doctoral degree, *Digital Urban Imaginaries*, from the University of Applied Arts Vienna, Austria, receiving the state prize from the Austrian Federal Minister of Science and Education. His work is bridging research and practice in the field of architecture and urban-design, co-developing *EnerPol* software for large-scale urban simulations. Currently, he is leading the Urban Transformation Project Sarajevo / Digital Twin and teaching at ETH Zürich and the University of Sarajevo Faculty of Architecture. During the opening of the 2023 Venice Architecture Biennale, he presented *Studio Mobil* as a dialogue platform for architecture, and human and environmental rights at the Global Campus of Human Rights in Venice.

Acknowledgements

The completion of this book was only possible thanks to collaboration and the help of many people. Aside from the collaborators, who dedicated a great deal of time to this guide, we would like to give special thanks to: Sloven Anzulović, Vedad Krkbešević, Sabina Hodović, Ivan Ramadan, Timur Babić for the various photos provided exclusively for this guide; Aleksandar Levi; Simone Voigt and Ajla Eljšani-Arnautlija from the Goethe-Institut Bosna i Hercegovina; Nina Ugljen-Ademović, Elša Turkušić, Nermina Zagora, Erdin Salihović from the Architectural Faculty Sarajevo; Danijela Dugandžić, Boriša Mraović, and Andreja Dugandžić from the Crvena organisation; Ognjenka Finci, Tatjana Neidhardt, Vesna Hercegovac-Pašić, Adnan Zvonić, Ervin Prašljivić, and all of the architectural studios and their photographers that have contributed to this book and the Days of Architecture Sarajevo archive.

The *Deutsche Nationalbibliothek* lists this
publication in the *Deutsche Nationalbibliografie*;
detailed bibliographic data are available at
http://dnb.d-nb.de.

ISBN 978-3-86922-381-0

© 2023 by DOM publishers, Berlin
www.dom-publishers.com

First reprint 2025

Authors' Note
This guide is an attempt to document part
of the architecture in Sarajevo in the past
100 years. However, it was not always possible
to find the complete names of all authors and
to find complete data or accurate information.
If readers can provide missing information,
please contact the publisher. It would be highly
appreciated, and it will be added in subsequent
editions of the book.

Proofreading
Sandie Kestell

Graphic Design
Dani Tecthour

Final Artworks
Masako Tomokiyo

QR-Codes
Irfan Salihagic

Printing
Drukarnia READ ME, Łódź
readme.pl